T

The Right Reverend John Flack
Honorary Assistant Bishop in the Church of England

6 Oakhall Park
Crigglestone   Tel: 01924 259 073
WAKEFIELD   Mobile: 07810 714 056
West Yorkshire, WF4 3HG   E-mail: johnflack67@yahoo.com

The Table

Knowing Jesus: Prayer, Friendship, Justice

Paul Bayes

+John – with love, thanks
and profound respect,
+Paul.

DARTON · LONGMAN + TODD

First published in 2019 by
Darton, Longman and Todd Ltd
1 Spencer Court
140–142 Wandsworth High Street
London SW18 4JJ

© 2019 Paul Bayes

ISBN 978-0-232-53372-9

Thanks are due to the following for permission to quote copyright material:
Victor Gollancz for *The Just Vengeance* by Dorothy L. Sayers; Faber and Faber
Limited for 'The Incarnate One' by Edwin Muir, taken from *Collected Poems*
by Edwin Muir.

A catalogue record for this book is available from the British Library.

Phototypeset by Kerrypress Ltd, Markyate, St Albans
Printed and bound in Great Britain by Bell & Bain, Glasgow

Contents

Preface

Images and ideas grow in the mind, and grow further as they are shared. This little book takes one such image, the image of the carpenter's table. It sets out to answer the question, What might it mean for the way we live and pray and act to see the Christian Church as an open table of friends, sitting beside One who calls and sends them in love?

I am grateful to the Diocese of Liverpool and to the Church of England for the three months' study leave which gave me the opportunity to rest, and learn, and write. Most of that study leave was spent in the United States, and I have enjoyed the generous hospitality of the Episcopal Church in a number of dioceses and institutions of learning. It is good to be in Communion with these friends and colleagues.

The Church is full of wonderful images, ideas and theological wisdom, from which I try to learn daily as I read and reflect. Among them I offer the perspectives here, as a contribution to the Church's storehouse.

Acknowledgements

I am very grateful to Mike Eastwood of the Diocese of Liverpool, to our Archdeacons and staff colleagues there, and to Nichola James, Sarah James and Phil Leigh who sustained the life of the bishop's office in my absence. Thanks too to Bishop Richard Blackburn who held the episcopal focus of the Diocese while I was away.

In California I was grateful to Dean Mark Richardson of the Church Divinity School of the Pacific, Berkeley, CA, for his welcome and that of his colleagues (especially Susanna Singer and Scott MacDougall), to Jude Harmon and the staff at Grace Cathedral San Francisco for a taste of their innovative ministries, and to Paul Fromberg and Rick Fabian of St Gregory of Nyssa parish for shared meals and for their gifts of wisdom and courage. Grace Flint welcomed me to California and kindly introduced this Brit to the life of the Bay Area.

It was very good to revisit Alexandria, VA, where Dean Ian Markham of Virginia Theological Seminary, Dr Robert Heaney of the Centre for Anglican Communion Studies, and Molly O'Brien of the CACS office, were kind and thoughtful hosts as ever.

In New York the Presiding Bishop of the Episcopal Church, Michael Curry, was most generous with his time, as were his colleagues Canon Chuck Robertson and David Copley. Elizabeth Boe greatly facilitated and enriched my stay right across the US, and introduced me to Holy Cross monastery which is a heartbeat of the Episcopal Church. Liz Edman, Matt Heyd and Nigel Massey kindly shared their thinking and wisdom with me. Matthew Corkern and the people of Calvary, Summit, New Jersey, gave me a nourishing taste of the rich local life and ministry of the Episcopal Church.

Part of the chapter Stretching for the Kingdom first appeared in *Journeys in Grace and Truth: Revisiting Scripture and Sexuality,* a collection of essays edited and animated by Jayne Ozanne. I take this opportunity to acknowledge my thanks to Jayne, and many others in the LGBTI+ community, for their courageous witness in and to the churches.

Six of my friends read this book in draft, and improved it. My thanks then to Nikki Eastwood, Richard Giles, Susan Goff, Paula Gooder, Stephen Lyon and Richard Peers.

David Moloney, Helen Porter and their colleagues at Darton, Longman and Todd have enabled the publication of this book, and in the process have enriched and deepened it.

None of these people is responsible for what I have written here, though many of them have inspired my thinking.

Kate Bayes is my lifelong friend and inspiration, with whom I have shared a table for more than forty years. I dedicate this book to her.

+Paul Liverpool
Alexandria, Virginia
Feast of St Gregory the Great[1]

Part I

1. So there's this table

*The inaugural sermon preached by the new Bishop of Liverpool,
November 2014.*

So there's this table.

It's a simple table but it's well made, because it was made by a
carpenter. The guy who made it is a poor man, but he's generous.
He offers a place at the table to anyone who wants to sit and eat.
This is a table that started in one place but now it can stretch down
every street, and it can go into every home, if people want to sit
there.

It's a table for meeting. It's a table for talking around. It's a table
for laughing. Most of all it's a table for eating. It's a level table. Maybe
it's not a round table. Maybe it's a square table, so that people can
look directly at one another as they sit there. Can look each other
in the eye as they sit there, beside the poor man who made it.

But it's not a high table. You don't have to qualify to sit there. It's
for anyone. And the poor man sits there, and wherever people sit, he
sits beside them. You can sit there too, with the poor man, and look
across the table, at people you like and at people you don't like, at
people who agree with you and at people who disagree with you.

Sometimes it's a table for thumping. Sometimes it's a table for
signing treaties and for making peace. Always the poor man sits
beside you.

Yes, most of all it's a table for eating. You can't eat alone at this
table. You can't buy a meal at this table. You can't buy a ticket to sit
here. Anyone can sit here. It's a table like a table at a wedding. You
sit with guests you never knew, and you find out about them, and
they become your friends. And the table is spread with a beautiful
fair white linen cloth and if you come here, like any pilgrim coming
into a new house, they will clothe you in the most beautiful clothes[1]
and they will make you welcome.

And if you eat the food served here you will never be hungry
again. Because the poor man offers the food at this table. And the

poor man will serve you, and the poor man's hands are wounded when he serves you, because the food came at a price, and he paid the price.

The poor man's name is Jesus, who though he was rich, yet for our sakes he became poor so that through his poverty we might become rich. And if you sit at his table he will feed you and he will ask you to feed others; he will serve you and he will ask you to serve others; he will love you and he will ask you to love others.

I'm a churchwarden's son and a cradle Christian, and I threw it all away in the late 1960s and early 70s to go my own way. And I was brought back to Christ through the ministry of student evangelists, and a radical Christian group, and a large suburban charismatic church, and a small inner-city Anglo-Catholic church, and a cathedral which was always open, and two professors of theology. One day if you ask me I'll tell you the full story. But using all those places and people, Jesus led me back to his table, and he leads me back still. As our sister Tracey[2] says in her words at the back of our Cathedral church, so I can say to the poor man, Jesus; 'I felt you and I knew you loved me'. So I did sit and eat and for fifty-three years off and on I have known him and he has never done me any harm. And for me he will be the first and the last word always.

My brother Malcolm[3] and my brother Phil[4] read this earlier; prophecies about Jesus:

'I will put my Spirit upon him, and he will proclaim justice to the Gentiles.'

And then:

'He will not wrangle or cry aloud until he brings justice to victory. And in his name the peoples will hope.'

And all this, the table and the poor man and justice brought to victory, all this is my vision of the church of Jesus Christ. A mixed group of ordinary people with the most extraordinary gift to share. And because the gift is so marvellous, that's why I want the church to grow. Not so that we can have a bigger church, but so that we can make a bigger difference. So that the poor man's table may be laid in every street. I want every church to grow.

The church does not grow so that it can survive. It is not our survival that matters. The church matters because Jesus matters, he who wants everyone's company, he who built the church on a rock, he who wants the table to be laid in every street.

The growth of the Church is a good in itself. We share the news about Jesus Christ so that people can come to know Him, and knowing Him is very good. So because I want people to hear the name of Jesus I want the Church to grow, because the poor Christ wants their company. That's why I'm committed to our mixed economy of parish churches and fresh expressions of the church, a people who can bring from their storehouse both the new and the old, so that all might know Jesus, the poor carpenter and the beautiful shepherd who is so ancient and so new.

Now is a good time for all this. The Church of England used to be in a spiritually dangerous place: we were cushioned by privilege, we were in the middle of our society and at the top. Now, in this England, we're on the edge and underneath - marginalised, not always taken seriously, sometimes mocked. That's good news for us. Because on the edge and underneath is where the people are.

Pope Francis says: '*An evangelising community gets involved by word and deed in people's daily lives; it bridges distances, it is willing to abase itself if necessary, and it embraces human life, touching the suffering flesh of Christ in others.*' The Bishop of Rome's vision is my vision for the church among the churches, for all the churches, as we gather again on the edge.

From the edge we give our gift, the knowledge of Jesus. Oh, that all people might know Him, and the power of His resurrection. Man and woman, rich and poor, gay and straight, black and white, conservative and progressive, believer and unbeliever, Jesus longs for our company. And his welcome is absolute.

The growth of the Church is a good in itself. But then those who sit at the poor man's table are called to follow their host. Jesus, who proclaimed justice, and who brought justice to victory.

In this region (Liverpool and Merseyside) we know about justice. It does not come without a struggle. It can take a long time. It demands patience, and the utmost truthfulness. We have the example of the Hillsborough families,[5] of their quiet perseverance and their patient and courageous refusal to be distracted or to despair.

And it is a matter of great pride to me that I walk in the footsteps of Bishop James who sought to serve those families and the memory of the ninety-six, and who in this Cathedral church presented a little of that story of truth. And I honour Bishop James, and Bishop David before him[6], and all those with them who sat at the poor man's table and who seek justice for the downtrodden. I am borne up by their memory.

And I stand here now as part of the poor man's community of justice. A bishop is always in the midst of a people, that's why I asked our Synod to accompany me up the hill from the centre of the city to the Cathedral today. I do not arrive on my own. I stand in the midst of the poor man's people and we are a people of justice, and from every community and every church we know those who care for the hungry and the needy and who speak for them and who lift their heads, and in the midst of you I commit myself to support you and to pray for you and to do what I can to be with you in that struggle.

Because this too is my vision of the church – a group of people who know Jesus and who proclaim justice. Because it is Jesus, we will not turn away from justice. Because it is Jesus, we will not wrangle or cry aloud or break the broken or ignore those who struggle. When I was involved as an activist in the peace movement of the 80s and 90s we had a saying, 'there is no way to peace – peace is the way'. Peace, and telling the truth.

In that spirit we in the church are called to approach our own troubles and disagreements. I do not seek a pure church if the price of a pure church is that our sisters and brothers are excluded, if the price of a pure church is a smaller table. The growth of the Church is a good in itself, so long as the poor Christ sits beside each one of us at His table and teaches us to love.

And I promise you – we will be there for you, for all, to walk and work with you in the way of peace, to spread the table of love, until our God brings justice to victory. And in the poor man's name the peoples will hope.

Jesus, may your name be first and last in all we say and do; and draw us to your Father in the power of the Spirit. Bring justice to victory. We ask this in your name, Jesus.

2. The banqueting table

He brought me to the banqueting table, and his banner over me is love.[1]

From the beginning God made people to share God's own life of love, and in living that life together to find their true selves, and God's purpose for them. This common life changes form with times and places, but it is one life, because God wishes people of all times and places to become one in God.[2]

The possibility of a way

As a child and then as a student I asked Jesus to meet me and to help me accept his love. Since then I have seen in Christianity the possibility of a way, just as St Luke reported in the Acts of the Apostles. You step on to it through a very specific door, as Jesus said, because it has to do with knowing Jesus personally. But if you walk along it, you find that it's a spacious, light, open and tolerant way, trusting and relaxed in the mystery of God and vibrant with hope for the world God loves.

At the heart of Christianity is this mystery and hope. When I was a theological student in the 1970s our college had a visit from the theologian David Jenkins, later Bishop of Durham. Bishop David was a great scholar and a profoundly orthodox theologian. He took off his jacket, rolled up his shirtsleeves, and began his lecture by saying: 'As I get older, I find I'm believing more and more about less and less'. And he summed up his more-and-more faith in this short phrase: *God is, as God is in Jesus, so there is hope*.

God is, as God is in Jesus, so there is hope. It's a phrase which does justice to the mystery of God about which the early theologians wrote so passionately. It honours the search for a better future which has marked our faith since its beginning. I've tried to give my life to the mystery and hope at the heart of Christianity, which is all to do with Jesus, over the last fifty years and more. I have tried to walk in this way, to discover the practical steps which are involved in walking in any way.

I've done this because the mystery and hope of Jesus grasped me and set the compass of my life. I chose to walk that way, but it has also been my experience that the way came to me, that Jesus chose me, poor and inadequate as my response to his choice has been. Jesus chose me to be one of his friends, and I said yes to his choice, not least because I had seen and known people walking this way too, people who were friends of his, people whose lives were shaped by this mystery and this hope.

They are everywhere. People living their lives in such a way that the life would make no sense if God, as God is in Jesus, did not exist. Among all the clouds and shadows that regularly gather around the institution of the Church, these people point to, and drink from, the living stream. I want to be like them, and I want to be like Jesus who gives them strength and to whom they point. I want there to be more of those people. I want to see their calm and vibrant hope translated into the celebration of justice and love for all, and into the ceaseless struggle for more justice and more love. In that struggle I want to learn especially from the excluded and those on the edge of things, and as I learn from them I want to stand with them.

In short, I want to see more people knowing Jesus, and more justice in the world. And I aim to stand with all those who want either or both of those things too.

Of course, you can be a Christian and not yet see the need to learn from and stand with those on the edge of things, 'the poor' as Jesus called them in the Gospels. If you are, I hope you will let me stand beside you. But you need to know that I will be stretching and reaching beyond my own comfort zone, and beyond the temporary walls that the people of God have built. I will stretch and reach to extend my love, and our love, so that it can be closer to the fully extended love of God – the fully extended love that brings all things to reconciliation in the end.

And of course, you can fight for justice without being a Christian, or indeed a person of religious faith at all. If you do, I want to stand beside you. But you need to know that I will stand with you as a follower of Jesus, and that I will be glad of his name and his mark, and I will speak of it. Because alongside the hope for a better world that we would share, I believe too in a mystery of love beyond the world. I believe that we live in a creation, and we are borne up by a love, that will not end when this world ends.

Love is the meaning

It is that love which gives meaning to things, as that tough and gentle woman Julian of Norwich wrote all those years ago:

> Do you want to understand your Lord's meaning in this experience? Understand it well: love was his meaning. Who showed it to you? Love. What did he show you? Love. Why did he show it? For love. Hold yourself in this truth and you shall understand and know more in the same vein. And you will never know or understand anything else in it forever.
>
> Thus was I taught that love is our Lord's meaning. And I saw most certainly in this and in everything that before God made us he loved us, and this love never slackened and never shall. In this love he has done all his works, in this love he has made all things profitable for us, and in this love our life is everlasting. In our creation we had a beginning, but the love by which he made us was in him from without beginning, and in this love we have our beginning. And all this we shall see in God without end.[3]

If love is the meaning, if love is indeed Jesus' meaning, I expect to see more people knowing Jesus and more justice in the world. I'll work for that. I'll work to see the increase of the people of Jesus and the willing and passionate inclusion of those on the edges; in short to see a bigger church that makes a bigger difference. I'll work to see a world where all human beings flourish; a world where the strong use their strength to honour others and not to put them down, to lift others up and not to trample them under. With all my strength I aim to advocate for such a world, and to bless and join those who are building it.

Christianity is a simple and a practical thing. It's a thing that you do before being a thing that you think. At least it has been so for me. In the Gospels the ones who follow Jesus are sent out, and the thing they are sent out to notice and grow is 'the Kingdom of God here among you', and the thing they are sent out to say is 'Come and see'. They, and we, are sent in other words to point to the real hope, and to introduce people to the true mystery.

The great Orthodox thinker Alexander Schmemann wrote once about preaching, and had a contrast to make:

> The genuine sermon is neither simply an explanation of what was read by knowledgeable persons, nor a transmission to the listeners of the theological knowledge of the preacher … It is not a sermon about the gospel, but the preaching of the gospel itself. [4]

That speaks to me of the Christian life as a whole. It is God who gives life to the dying. It is the living spark, rather than a treatise on light, which will prevent people from stumbling. It is the living bread that nourishes; and though menus can look lovely with their paper and card and print, no one would want to eat one. As St Paul sharply and perhaps ruefully reflects from the perspective of his own Pharisaic training, 'Knowledge makes people arrogant, but love builds people up'. He goes on to lay out the paradox, which in today's church we hear insufficiently: 'If anyone thinks they know something, they don't yet know as much as they should know. But if someone loves God, then they are known by God'. [5] And of course, this raises the sharp question, how? How do we get real and true? What sort of communication, what sort of life, is needed for that?

The question came back again to me, sharper than ever, when I was asked to be the bishop of a Diocese in the Church. I was invited to speak to the appointed group of people, and to answer questions, so that they might discern whether I should be invited to be Bishop of Liverpool. The date for the conversation was April Fools' Day 2014 - a date which explains a lot, or so the people of Liverpool might think.

Four years before that, I had become a suffragan bishop in the Diocese of St Albans. I was an ordained Christian minister for thirty-one years before I became a bishop. And I am infinitely grateful to God and God's people to have become a bishop in the Church. Episcopal ministry came to me as a gift and a surprise, and I received it with the utmost delight and thanksgiving. I didn't expect to be a bishop, and you can't ask to be one. And I frequently pinch myself when I remember that I am one.

And of all the places where you can be a bishop, I thank God daily that I have been a bishop in Liverpool. Together with the strong and courageous towns around it, our city region is made up of people who endure, who are humorous, unbowed by poverty and suffering, tough, resilient, emotional, full of faith, who love justice and the struggle for justice. The ordained and lay ministers of our Diocese and of our sister churches (and many of them have chosen to give their whole lives to this region and its people) share these qualities, even as they live out the mystery and the hope of their calling in worship and service day by day and decade by decade. To stand among them is an overwhelming joy.

All this was in the future when I was asked to interview, but I saw it dimly and I felt the question sharply; what sort of communication, what sort of life, is needed to enrich and honour and bless such extraordinary people?

Singing a song

My name is Leah. I love to help people and sing.[6]

I believe that the purpose of leadership in the Church (and not only in the Church) is basically twofold: to sing a song and to get a grip. The ministry of bishops touches both these things, just as both are also shared with colleagues and no one can or should be expected to do all the work of Christian leadership alone.

There are many occasions in the life of the Church where it helps to get a grip. I have done so myself, and I deeply respect and honour my colleagues who do so daily as the core of their ministry. But for me the primary ministry of bishops flows from the singing of the song, the love-song of the Christian gospel. Episcopacy is a lyric art, rather than an academic science. So when I was interviewed, and still more when I began to prepare for my public ministry, it was a lyric that I needed, a song of love, a song full of images, like the images Jesus used in his own lyrical teaching, like the images the Church has used ever since.

Images of the Christian life come into and go out of fashion over the years. There are plenty to be found in scripture, and in the history of the Church. They emerge and recede according to the social context, though many of them recur as the high images of our tradition; for example, the body of Christ, the army of God, the pilgrim people, the temple, the bride.

But as I thought and prayed at that moment in my own journey, the image that came to me was none of these, though it was not original. It has been used frequently in the history of our faith and it's used frequently now. It was the image of a table – specifically the table of a poor carpenter, at which the carpenter sits beside any who sit there. And having been appointed, I laid this image of the carpenter's table before my Diocese when I began my ministry in Liverpool, in the sermon which forms the previous chapter here. And I invited myself and all my companions to come to this table, to the table of the wounded Christ, and to be seated beside him, beside the poor carpenter. Sitting there we meet him and are fed by him, and we are called by him to pray, and read, and learn at the holy table, and we are sent by him to tell, and serve, and give from the open table.

That image of the carpenter's table is the heart of this book. In that sermon I tried to spread the table before my friends and colleagues and companions. By this image I tried to put into words some implications of the astonishing mystery and hope we see in Jesus. I tried to say how it might be to live and to walk in the way I long for, in a spacious, light, open and tolerant way, trusting and relaxed in the mystery of God and vibrant with hope for the world God loves.

Scandal

To sit at a table is a common enough experience, though in these fragmented, TV-dinner days it is perhaps not as common as it should be. Jesus did it frequently, and almost as frequently it landed him in hot water with people who were keen on the difference between right and wrong. St Luke is the gospel writer who notices this most often. Sometimes Jesus was sitting at the wrong table (for example the table of the crooked tax collector Zacchaeus).[7] Sometimes he was at the right table, but in the wrong company (for example at Simon the Pharisee's table, with a notorious woman washing his feet).[8] Sometimes he was at the right table, but saying and doing the wrong thing (for example at another Pharisee's table, ritually unwashed and full of sharp words for his hosts and their arrogance).[9]

The capacity of Jesus to scandalise people was legendary, and in human terms it cost him first his freedom and then his life. It is at least arguable that the real focus of this scandal was not what he said in the public square but where he ate and with whom, and what he did at the table. Certainly, this is the view of the radical New Testament theologian John Dominic Crossan, who contrasts Jesus and John the Baptist by quoting the words of their enemies:

> John fasted and they called him demonic; Jesus ate and drank and they said he was 'a glutton and a drunkard, a friend of tax collectors and sinners.'

Lk
14
15

He goes on to comment on Jesus' parable of the banquet, which comes among several other table-stories in Luke 14 and 15:

> What Jesus' parable advocates, therefore, is an 'open commensality', an eating together without using the table as a miniature map of society's vertical discriminations and lateral separations.[10]

In San Francisco there is an inspirational local church, St Gregory of Nyssa, where St Luke's emphasis has become the guiding emphasis of the community. The altar greets those who enter the church; if they want to see the font, they must pass through the church to a rocky outcrop behind it. That prominent and open altar carries more words from Luke, this time in Greek from chapter 15. The words are translated by one of its founding priests and theologians, Rick Fabian, as follows:

> 'This guy welcomes sinners and eats with them.'[11]

The other side of that altar carries words from St Isaac of Nineveh:

> Did not the Lord share the table of tax collectors and harlots? So then – do not distinguish between the worthy and unworthy. All must be equal in your eyes to love and to serve.[12]

In the gospels of course Jesus was a wanderer, you might say a vagrant. He did not have a table of his own, nor a place to lay his head. When he sat it was as a guest at the tables of others. But the mystery of our faith is that we can now sit at his table, the table of the poor carpenter built by the Spirit, the table that can change us utterly. It's not always a warm and cosy table, and sometimes he sets it up in the most uncomfortable places, in the streets where the lonely walk and on the beaches where the refugees' boats wait, and in the prison yards and in the cancer wards and in the graveyards. But for those who choose to sit there it will always be the right table, that is Jesus' table, and we will always be in the right company; that is, among friends, among all the wrong people, hearing the gentle words of the One who offers rest, and whose yoke is easy and whose burden is light.

The spacious and open way leads to this table and leads from it, and we are welcome there, just as all are welcome there. The poor man who constructed the table is also the Shepherd, the Beautiful One, who knows us and whom we know.[13] Strangers and the despised are welcome at this table, especially welcomed by those who remember the Name of the crucified carpenter, and who can say with the people of St Gregory of Nyssa:

> Blessed be God the Word, who came to his own and his own received him not, for in this way God glorifies the stranger. Oh God, show us your image in all we meet today that we may welcome them, and you, through Jesus Christ our Lord. Amen.[14]

From all this I hope you will see the richness and the depth of this image of the table, and the catchiness of the song that builds a life on it. As I have reflected on that image, I think that it can take its place as the fountainhead of a stream of Christian practice. Seeing the church as a table of welcome can form the lives of twenty-first-century believers along the pattern laid out in scripture and in the writings of the early theologians of the Way. And certainly, this way of seeing – of seeing the church as a table of welcome – is present today as a living stream in the Church, even if it is often, as it has always been, an underground stream.

Practice

I feel the need to say these things for a reason. These days the attractiveness and beauty of Jesus is not always seen and understood beyond the Church. The preoccupations, indeed the obsessions, of

Christians are not always respected or found interesting by those who live in the world for which the poor carpenter died. This is a daily concern for me, as it is for anyone who bears the burden of the churches.

This is why I speak about 'Christian practice' rather than outlining yet more divisive ways for us to be 'clear' about our 'teaching'. In reflecting on these things in the UK and in the USA, I've come very firmly to believe that 'poor little talkative Christianity' can only point to Jesus' attractiveness and beauty in the world if its people stop attacking and defending one another for a while, and instead practise their religion, preferably together. Like the stranger in Dostoyevsky's tale of the Grand Inquisitor, the poor and imprisoned Jesus will kiss the bloodless lips of the doctrine police, and set even them free to sit at the table and to eat with the rest.

Beginning with the table, then, these chapters seek to explore what Christian practice looks like today. I'll point to a number of traditions and ways of living and believing, most of them embraced in the wide arms of the Anglican Communion. But I have no particular steer to give, within that wide embrace, as to whether any specific ways are to be preferred to others. Instead I'm asking what the principles and marks of Christian practice should be, across the Church. The practices I describe and commend are not new; at least I hope not. They fall into four groups, and of the four, meeting at the table is the first and the foundation.

So, this is what I ask, as I practise singing the love-song of the Gospel and as I live within a world desperate for the mystery and hope that the song bears. Can we practise together in these four ways? Can we meet at the table, first and foremost? And drink from the fountain? And watch in the moment? And stretch for the kingdom?

Thank you then for picking up this book and for beginning, at least, that journey of enquiry with me.

3. The Lord's table

God is the interesting thing about religion, and people are hungry for God.[1]

God, who made the world and everything in it, is Lord of heaven and earth. He doesn't live in temples made with human hands. Nor is God served by human hands, as though he needed something, since he is the one who gives life, breath, and everything else. From one person God created every human nation to live on the whole earth, having determined their appointed times and the boundaries of their lands. God made the nations so they would seek him, perhaps even reach out to him and find him. In fact, God isn't far away from any of us. In God we live, move, and exist. As some of your own poets said, 'We are his offspring'.[2]

The invisible God

Mystery and hope stand at the heart of the Christian religion, and faith becomes vibrant and beautiful and compelling when we connect with the truth of this. And first there comes the mystery of God, the interesting thing about religion, who is closer to us than we are to ourselves, indeed who is out of our sight because so close.

In St Matthew's Gospel Jesus says, 'Look, I myself will be with you every day until the end of this present age'.[3] And in St John's Gospel it says, 'No one has ever seen God'.[4] We are invited to believe both these things. The closeness and invisibility of the undergirding God is a wonderful and a heart-breaking thing. Wonderful, because of the way it witnesses to God with us, to God's love offered unceasingly and universally, present in every moment and in every place. Heart-breaking, because coming to terms with the invisibility of God is difficult. Why can God not be more obvious? Our minds and hearts rebel at the unfairness of it. We find the invisible oddness of God's presence so difficult, indeed, that as God's people we have largely preferred not to think about it, nor to engage with it in our prayers. We seem to find it much easier to dispute with one another about the boundaries and fence-posts of God's love as expressed through our institutions, which are at least visible, than to seek the One we cannot see. And yet the interesting thing about religion is precisely that loving and invisible One.

Jesus was once as visible as I am now in the days of my life on this earth. And today with the eyes of faith we can see the traces and the presence of the ascended Jesus everywhere in the world, because of the promise of the Incarnation. Especially in the lives and lessons of those on the edge of things can we see the marks of Jesus, if we trust his own promise that he would be present among them. And in the sacrament of Holy Communion we can see him present, if we have faith in the promise of the scripture. There is a lot about God to be seen in the world. And yet still it is no part of the Christian mystery to see God here on earth, whom no one has ever seen.

So when we speak of mystery we are indicating nothing weird or exalted. We have in mind a different thing from highfalutin and other-worldly ideas of 'mystical vision'. Quite the contrary; it seems to me that 'religious experience', experience which is too markedly religious, has the effect of distracting people from the real world that God loves, and so in the end distracting them from the real God who loves it.

My own journey in faith, like anyone else's, has had to come to terms with this invisibility and its disappointments. God is at once more transcendent, and more utterly immanent, than I would wish. I would frankly prefer something more spooky and spine-tingling in my God. I would prefer the theophanies of Exodus and of the Psalms to be a daily or at least a regular occurrence, with thunder and lightning, 'hailstones and coals of fire'.

It would be particularly satisfying if the God of thunderbolts would not only appear, but would direct his thunderbolts against my enemies while I looked on. Why can God's action not be like the beautiful and terrible angels in *Raiders of the Lost Ark* who swirl around the moral arena, wreaking havoc and vengeance on all the bad people?

Elijah too might have hoped that God would reveal God's self in these ways, when he went and stood at the mouth of the cave and heard the thunder and saw the earthquake and the fire, 'but the LORD was not in' these things.[5] Instead we have a God in whom we live, move and exist.

At the table you sit close beside the poor carpenter Jesus, who has invited you and made room for you there. You are very close, you and he, sitting side by side and gazing in the same direction. If he were more distant from you, then you might turn and see him.

But he is close to you, closer to you than you think, closer indeed than you are to yourself. So you can turn as quickly as you like but you cannot see him with the eyes of your body. Since the day of his ascension no one ever has. And yet we, even you, even I, can be sitting right beside him at the table, because he has invited us and made room for us there.

Of course, we do not have to sit there. There is a choice in sitting, and there is a choice in looking. As we sit, then, we may choose to look in the same direction that the poor carpenter looks. Indeed, our growth in holiness is just that; a growth in seeing things that he sees, a development in our looking, a sharpening of our attention. If we choose to look his way, then for example we will see the needy and be drawn to meet their need. We will see the beauty of the earth and be drawn to sustain it. We will see those who sit opposite us at the table, and be drawn to speak truth to them and to love them as they really are.

Sitting and looking and acting; that is what it is to be a believer, and indeed as Aelred Squire says, 'Unless we approach him who is nearer to us than we are to ourselves, he might just as well not exist, as far as we are concerned'.[6] And as we look we realise finally that we have come to depend on the poor carpenter for food and life and strength even though, gazing in the same direction with him, we cannot see him. Yet as we look his way, then in the depth of our being, and solely by his grace, we know he is there, unseen. This is the mystery I mean.

The Christian Church is a wide and winding watercourse, meandering across the plains of history, now and again becoming lost in the salty marshlands of complacency, now and again becoming stagnant with internal politics and rank with contention. Yet always it has been fed by the living water, bubbling up in the midst of the dankest pools, springing from the edge and bursting from the rocks in the wilderness, bringing refreshment and nourishment, fulfilling the promises of the scripture that 'wherever the river flows, everything will live'.[7]

The underground stream

Early in the 1980s I worked as a University chaplain in London. A flat was provided with the job, in a well-off part of the city, in Campden Hill Square, Kensington. On the way home each day I would climb the hill, passing on the way the homes of the great and the good (Harold Pinter and Antonia Fraser, Tony Benn, the then Bishop of Kensington, the then editor of *The Times*). But at that time only one of the houses there had a blue plaque on the wall, at number 50: 'Evelyn Underhill 1875-1941, Christian philosopher and teacher'.

Evelyn Underhill was in many ways a typical upper-middle-class Englishwoman. Her father was a lawyer, and she eventually married another lawyer, and in her time that was all that was expected of most women – to be defined by the men in their lives, to sustain a social life, to bear children, to keep house. But there was much more than that to Evelyn Underhill. She thought and wrote about God in a way that was passionate and experiential and engaged, a way that expected God to be interesting and to be real. It was she who wrote to the Archbishop of Canterbury the words at the heart of this chapter: 'God is the interesting thing about religion, and people are hungry for God.'

In the days of Evelyn Underhill's life, by and large, the Church paid even less attention to the thinking and writing of lay Christian women than it does now. And of course, in my own church Christian women were 'lay women' by definition, until very recently. But from the heart of upper-middle-class London, Evelyn Underhill produced over thirty widely-read books, almost all about the mystery and glory of God, of which the best-known was called *Mysticism*. And people did indeed pay attention; the interesting thing interested them.

All through the life of the Christian Church there have been people like Evelyn Underhill, reminder-people who have lived on the edge of institutional power, who seem to have had little interest in the politics of the institution or the clash of its parties or factions, who wanted instead to take on themselves the mystery of things, as if they were God's spies. These are the people of the welling springs, the people of the living water. Most commonly they have been unseen and unknown in the days of their lives. Yet together their witness has become an underground stream in the life of the Church, invisible, running silently and deeply, fundamentally nourishing and enriching.

Frequently these reminder-people have been called mystics or have themselves used 'mysticism' as a description of what interests them, as Evelyn Underhill did. That in itself has been enough for them to be marginalised still further by the Church they felt called to serve, a Church which has so often suspected the mystical and which still does, worrying that it is unclear, or unsound, or uncontrollable. And one of my purposes in reflecting on all this is to demystify and democratise the mysterious, to which I believe God calls us all in love.

Very often the marginal reminder-people have been women. I am writing these words in Berkeley, California, in a small suite of rooms called the Dame Julian suite, so named in memory of another woman who pointed to God as the interesting thing. Dame (Mother) Julian, who lived and died centuries ago in Norwich, is honoured today in California and across the world Church for good reason. She was a significant contributor to the underground stream, this woman of the twelfth and thirteenth centuries who lived quietly, in solitude, suffering great physical pain. Out of her pain she felt that God's love had been shown to her, and she wrote about that and made herself available from her cell to listen to and counsel those who were caught in the pain and interested in the love. The cell still stands, on the edge of the historic centre of Norwich. It is close to several blocks of low-rise flats, and though most photographs of the church artfully exclude these, it is the presence of the flats more than anything which authenticates Julian's shrine for me, the shrine of an everyday woman of the city, a woman on the edge, unremarkable, utterly remarkable.

From here, from the edge of things and in pain, Julian wrote of the heart of things and of the meaning of things in blessedness. Earlier in this book I have paid attention to what she said. Here is more, for those who sit at the table - the mystery in the moment:

> It is easier for us to get to know God than to know our own soul ... God is nearer to us than our soul, for He is the ground

in which it stands ... so if we want to know our own soul, and
enjoy its fellowship, it is necessary to seek it in our Lord God.[8]

And the hope in the future:

For this is the Great Deed that our Lord shall do, in which
Deed He shall save His word and He shall make all well
that is not well. How it shall be done there is no creature
beneath Christ that knoweth it, nor shall know it till it is
done ...[9]

The witness of the underground stream, witnessing to the closeness
of God and the impetus of hope, almost always comes from the
edge and the edgy. Often, as I say, it comes from women – who have
indeed spent millennia on the edge – but not always. So for example,
Herbert Kelly was a maverick trainer of the clergy, the founder
of the Society of the Sacred Mission, committed to training and
equipping those without an Oxbridge education for the ministry
of the Church. One of his ordinands, an anxious young man, is
reported to have asked him what the point of ministry was, and
what he should be doing with his life. Kelly is said to have looked
at the young man in silence for a while, and then to have said, 'Oh,
sonny. Oh, sonny. People today only want to know one thing. Does
God do anything, and if so, what?'

The flowing of the underground stream is sustained and
unbroken in the long tradition of the Church, and indeed from
one point of view it constitutes the tradition itself. It is not reserved
for experts in the life of the spirit. It is the birthright of all believers,
the inheritance into which we can all come. Its engine is, and
will always be, the centrality of God, proclaimed from the edge by
people like Evelyn Underhill and Dame Julian and Herbert Kelly –
by people who do not fit the mould, people who are not expected,
people who come at things from a different angle, people who
know that God is first. And the life to which they witness remains
the interesting thing about religion.

God on the streets: justice and wonder

For some years I was privileged to work alongside the Archbishops
of Canterbury and York and a lively, creative and diverse group

of men and women whom they had drawn together, in the Archbishops' Task Group on Evangelism. The purpose of the Task Group was to support and resource the people of God in the sharing of their faith, and among other things to listen to England as it is, and to find out whether people were still interested.

As part of this listening the Group commissioned some research, from agencies whose usual work was commercial and industrial rather than purely academic. The commission was not 'market research', however, since the focus was not on the Church and its market share, but on God.

The work was done among particular groups of people who, statistically speaking, seem unimpressed with the Christian religion as it is presented to them these days. The focus was on young adults from lower-middle-class and working-class backgrounds who did not already see themselves as Christians. It is not hard to find people like this, since in this demographic the church is struggling and has been for decades.

So a number of young men and women were interviewed in the streets, most especially in the streets of Liverpool, and others were interviewed in specially-gathered small groups. The findings were partly expected and partly surprising, as the best research so often is. The researchers reported that their interviewees had little sympathy for the idea of an institutional Church, and furthermore (unlike a previous generation of unchurched people) that they did not see Jesus as a figure particularly worthy of their respect either. This is not because Jesus had lost their affection, but because they knew so little about him and never had, and because they assumed naturally enough that he must be like his followers who bore his name, and they found those followers negative, uncongenial and uninteresting.

But although Jesus no longer had purchase on their imagination, these people still had time and room for God, that is for 'something more', mysterious as that something was, and hard though it was for them to articulate it. The interesting thing contained to interest them. For themselves, and still more for their children, they wanted connection with that which they did not know.

Moreover, we were told that, although the interviewees' respect for the Church was slender, it came alive in two aspects of the life of Christians. The first was the involvement of the churches in practical and local issues of social justice (for example the running of food banks or the provision of debt advice, or (this was Liverpool) the advocacy of the Church for justice for the families of the victims of the Hillsborough disaster. And the second was the readiness of Christians to provide church buildings as places to go to for space, silence and peace.

Echoing my own words, mystery and hope, the Task Group's researchers came to us with two more from unchurched England: justice and wonder. These, they said, were the connection-points between England and its Church as their interviewees saw it. And the message of the people of Liverpool in 2015 has been echoed across the country in formal and informal research conducted elsewhere. The hunger expressed by so many beyond the community of faith is for justice and wonder. For that which is open and green, not cut and dried.

In common with the consensus of witness from many sources, our interviewees were almost unanimous in their distaste for the church as they understood it. To them it was a toxic brand. They had accepted the commonly-held caricature of Christianity; that it is a joyless, aridly intellectual, propositional, conceptual, legalistic system. They saw it as being better at defining than at opening; better at condemning than at loving; demanding correctness and soundness and agreement, deploring ambiguity or tolerance. In particular people outside the Church reported, and still report, that the Christian faith seems to them intrinsically misogynistic and homophobic, and they are unsurprised too if they see racism or abuse or the privileging of class or the sustaining of elites in the life of the community of faith. They simply did not know that at the heart of the Christian faith is a love that opposes all these things.

Truth and beauty

How can this woeful tale of suspicion be redeemed by the mystery and the hope at the heart of the Christian religion? How can the vibrant and beautiful and compelling dimensions of the life of faith, the living water of the underground stream, overcome the smoky and all-too-well-founded suspicions of our neighbours?

Not at any rate by ignoring the need for understanding truth about God, insofar as that has been revealed to us. The human condition can be explained by the teaching of the Church, and the narrative of our faith has not ceased to be compelling. We have a story to tell.

It is a beautiful and spacious story. That the world was made by God to be good; that we bear the image of God by His gift; that we have however lost the divine likeness because of the sin that preceded us and engulfs us and in which we now actively share personally and corporately; that our lostness and brokenness and the world's bewilderment can be redeemed because of what Jesus has done in coming among us, living and dying and rising and breathing the Spirit; that Jesus' self-giving love led him to the place of his dying; that the cross of Christ is indeed the test of everything, that for our eternal joy we depend radically on God's grace that comes to us though we do not deserve it; that at the end of time all will be well.

But we must face the fact that our faith simply does not look that way to very large numbers of people outside it. Beauty and spaciousness do not largely figure in the public conversations of the churches either, being replaced there by finger-wagging admonitions and critiques, from people whose time seems mostly to be spent in mutual disdain and in-fighting.

That the extraordinary and life-giving truths of the Faith have no purchase on the imagination of the unchurched West represents a profound relational failure on the part of the people of God. We have settled for what is narrow, mistaking our own narrowness for the narrow gate of which our Lord speaks.[10] And to reconnect with the attractiveness of the story we have a job to do. The art of Christian discipleship today must include the willingness to face, grip and dispel the caricatures, and the lamentable realities, of a supercilious condemnation.

We can do this if we use the real resources of our faith. And first among these resources is the beauty of the Christian life as it is actually lived. Christians believe that we speak the truth about God. But the way we say what is true determines whether it confers life. And we must know that all too often the content of the teaching can be nourishing and life-bearing, but the way the teaching is conferred can be toxic and death-dealing. As my father used to say, 'The truth is a sharp sword. You can kill more than falsehood with it.'

The US conservative commentator and Orthodox Christian Rod Dreher expresses this beautifully in an online dialogue:

> Jesus pointed to the boundaries within which Christians must live. He said clearly that he did not come to abolish the law, but to fulfil it. He also repeatedly made clear that one can be doctrinally correct and still be completely corrupt ('whitewashed tombs'). The purpose of religion is to convert the heart. If doctrine and dogma do not convert the heart and lead one closer to union with the All-Holy, then they are a stumbling block. Yet the absence of doctrine and dogma is also a stumbling block, because we are left without any idea what God 'looks like,' or expects us to become.[11]

We can indeed know what God looks like or expects us to become, as we embrace the embodied mystery of things within the community of faith. To do otherwise is to die in the propositional desert, endlessly chewing on thoughts and ideas as though they were food, constantly seeking to be right, by – how else to demonstrate rightness? – by proving others wrong.

Word and blood

In a sharp poem Edwin Muir spoke of the triumph of the propositional in religion, the triumph of a box-ticking rectitude, of cold words and thoughts over hot life and breath. Muir addresses 'King Calvin' from his own specific Scottish experience, which I do not share. But his sense echoes in poetry across the Christian world, echoing for example that of the Welsh Anglican R. S. Thomas, and I do not reproach him for his concreteness, and I stand with him in his uncompromising embrace of the incarnate One and his turning from the arid, disembodied, abstract word:

> … How could our race betray
> The Image, and the Incarnate One unmake
> Who chose this form and fashion for our sake?

> The Word made flesh here is made word again
> A word made word in flourish and arrogant crook.
> See there King Calvin with his iron pen,
> And God three angry letters in a book,
> And there the logical hook
> On which the Mystery is impaled and bent
> Into an ideological argument.[12]

I stand with this way of speaking, gladly welcoming mystery and living in hope. My life is given to the hospitable table of the poor carpenter (the one who was pilloried for being a party-goer) rather than to the classroom of the clever and severe schoolmasters. I want my friends to sit at the table, not be made to stand in the dunce's corner. For myself, I want to make the journey away from my primeval shame and fear of mortality to the table which has room for me and forever. I want these things for my own sake and for the sake of those who have missed Jesus because all they can see is the bone-dry valley of regulation, which for them has capped and polluted the wellspring of life.

Ours is indeed a faith based on God's revelation, but the God who is revealed in scripture and tradition and reason is a God greater than we can read about or remember or grasp.

So the Bible says that Jesus is the Son of God. But of God it says, 'Truly, you are a God who hides himself, O God of Israel, the Saviour',[13] and again: 'Without any doubt, the mystery of our religion is great',[14] and again of Jesus himself, 'among you stands one you do not know'.[15]

The theologians of the early Church, clear and accurate as they sought to be, had little time for the cut and dried. The great theologians of Cappadocia for example moved confidently through the philosophical controversies of their day, but Gregory of Nyssa speaks for them all when he says, 'Concepts create idols of God, of whom only wonder can tell us anything', and who went on with a familiar and rueful bitterness to acknowledge, 'People kill one another over idols. Wonder makes us fall to our knees.[16]' The anonymous Midlander who wrote *The Cloud of Unknowing* could say of God, 'He may well be loved, but not thought. By love may He be gotten and holden; but by thought never'.[17] Standing much later in time but immersed in the same underground stream, Thomas Merton could say drily: 'If you find God with great ease, perhaps it is not God you have found'.

Reason too finds itself debating inconclusively whether reason has its limits, and some of the greatest exponents of reason find themselves unashamedly speechless in the face of mystery and hope. So Isaac Newton and Thomas Aquinas, separated by so much culturally, were each reduced to wonder in remarkably similar ways, so that Newton's 'To myself I am only a child playing on the beach, while vast oceans of truth lie undiscovered before me' chimes with Aquinas' statement, 'The end of my labours has come, and all that I have written appears to be as so much straw after the things that have been revealed to me.'

Theology and prayer

Scripture and tradition and reason, the great sources of the Anglican way, leave room for mystery and hope at every turn. None of this is new insight, though speaking specifically as a bishop it seems necessary from time to time to remember it and to speak of it, since it can so easily be forgotten in the harsh sparkle of over-polished clarities, the raucous clash of concept and law which so often passes for conversation in the churches.

But there is a quieter and more convincing voice. We can be open to others and to the world; we can be gentle in the face of adversity; we can enjoy a simple gladness in the face of grace and love; we can choose to endure and to forgive and to celebrate diversity and beauty. All these things are directly related to our daily-renewed connection with the mystery of God - that is to say, our living experience of dependence on the mystery revealed as love.

The attractiveness of people of faith seems to be in inverse proportion to their sense that they have nailed down exactly what God is up to. And the lovely thing is that there is room for this attractiveness in our tradition, room for a lively sense of mystery leading to a living hope, room for mystery and hope together leading to life.

And people who think and live this way are everywhere, revived by the underground stream in the Church, quietly and courteously sharing the living water with those around them who are thirsty, water-carriers around whom are more people knowing Jesus, more justice in the world.

We need to hear their witness. Because those of us who sit at the table of the poor carpenter Jesus can always be distracted into long, involved and scholarly debates about what we do, rather than who God is. We will talk and talk about our own contributions to the wholly sufficient gifts of God; about the tablecloth we have added to the table, or about the kind of knife and fork we have bought and decided how to use, or about the font we have used on the menu we have printed.

Often these conversations are dignified with the word 'theological'. 'Theology' is a straightforward word that means 'talk about God'. But in parts of today's church it seems to have become tribal, owned and used as a weapon by those with a particular approach, part of an irregular verb in the combative mood: 'I am theological, you have not read quite enough, he/she/they are ignorant'. Similarly the phrase 'we need to do further theological work on this' can too often be a synonym for 'I don't like this outcome, and I want to postpone any decision on it'.

In *Asking the Fathers* Aelred Squire tells a story that redeems and reclaims the word 'theologian' for the whole people of God. He speaks of the eleventh-century woman St Gertrude of Helfta, who in her *Revelations* tells the story of her life, how she received what we would call a liberal education which equipped her to be what she calls a 'grammarian', someone who could use grammar and culture and language and thought to good effect. Gertrude goes on to tell of an experience of depression and soul-sickness which culminated in and was healed 'in the dormitory after Compline on the last Monday in January, in a totally unabated encounter with our Lord'. This experience of being unmade by God, of being in the presence of infinite mystery, opens up to Gertrude the depth of life, what you might call the abyss of love. Aelred Squire sums up the effect in these words:

> What matters is not so much the nature of the encounter…
> but its effect, which tradition is unanimous in regarding as
> the only sure test of an experience of this kind. This effect

> Gertrude's friend and biographer describes in a simple phrase.
> It was thus, she says, that from being a grammarian she became
> a theologian.[18]

'She became a theologian.' She became one whose culture and language and thought came into orbit around God, and the mystery of God.

No degree is needed for such a shift, no formal accreditation. You don't need to identify yourself with a party in the Church, or go hunting for others to 'critique'. There is no need to give long words too much room in the mind. Instead, there is dependence on God's mystery, in prayer. From that dependence, people of all academic abilities and of all cultures can sit at the table and speak of God with authenticity and in truth. Without that dependence, 'theology' is just another weapon, a way of scoring points and playing games; at its best like chess, at its worst like bullying.

In the fourth century the monk Evagrius said: 'If you are a theologian you truly pray. If you truly pray you are a theologian.'[19] It is the Lord's table where we sit, and even if it sometimes seems that little attention is paid at the table by the often-squabbling diners, nonetheless it is God that matters, the God of mystery and hope – and anything else only matters because it points to God, or because it comes from God who points to us, or from God who points us to something beyond ourselves. God is the interesting thing about religion; God who is real and whose mystery is given to us, to be honoured and entered and shared.

4. The daily table

Whoever wants to do God's will can tell whether my teaching is from God or whether I speak on my own.[1]

Love doesn't just sit there, like a stone; it has to be made, like bread, remade all the time, made new.[2]

Thinking and doing

Christianity is lived in the act of being believed, or you might say Christianity is believed as it is lived. In some ways Christianity is lived before it is believed. This is because Christianity is a religion. It is unfashionable to say this today, but that does not make it untrue.

'Religion' has had a bad name in the past few decades. It's come under attack on two fronts. Firstly it comes off poorly in the phrase 'spiritual but not religious', which large numbers of people outside the churches have used to describe themselves. The phrase opposes spirituality (good) and religion (bad). In the minds of the unchurched people who speak like this, 'spiritual' seems to be a heart thing, and a gentle one, to be accepted; while 'religion' seems to be a head thing, and a harsh and critical one, to be rejected. And goodness knows, many of these people have stories to tell, usually stories of specific rejections within the general unwelcome of the church as they have known it – stories that have given them ample reason to think this way.

And secondly 'religion' gets a kicking from some in the Church itself because (they rightly say) Jesus came to abolish legalistic, ritual, ceremonial ways to appease an angry and glowering God, and so (they wrongly say) 'Christianity is just about relationship, and not about religion'.

Christianity is indeed about relationship. That is wonderful, and undeniable. God subverts and undermines all religious systems, and this is so throughout the scriptures. In the prophecy of Ezekiel we see the underground stream surfacing, in a startling image of a church with divine water damage, one guaranteed to disconcert heritage societies, churchwardens and Archdeacons alike:

> When he brought me back to the temple's entrance, I noticed that water was flowing toward the east from under the temple's threshold (the temple faced east). The water was going out from under the temple's facade toward the south, south of the altar. He led me out through the north gate and around the outside to the outer east gate, where the water flowed out under the facade on the south side. With the line in his hand, the man went out toward the east. When he measured off fifteen hundred feet, he made me cross the water; it was ankle-deep. He measured off another fifteen hundred feet and made me cross the water; it was knee-deep. He measured off another fifteen hundred feet and made me cross the water, and it was waist-high. When he measured off another fifteen hundred feet, it had become a river that I couldn't cross. The water was high, deep enough for swimming but too high to cross. He said to me, 'Human one, do you see?'[3]

God, the interesting thing about religion, is not to be put in a pipe. The underground stream will wear away the hardest rock. For myself I thank God that the Lord Jesus came to meet me in my lostness and came to save me from my sinfulness. I thank God that the radical message of Jesus has never been completely stifled by the power-games that his people play, and that the living water continues to flow out from beneath the threshold of the temple, becoming a river that cannot be crossed or stifled or dammed. But with all that, I thank God too that Christianity is a religion, and that I can practice it.

This is because I am definitely a practising Christian. Practising, because I haven't got it right. And practising, because Christianity is a daily thing. We sit at the table, daily. We meet God and one another, daily. We drink from the fountain and watch in the moment and stretch for the Kingdom, anew every morning.

The gentle and open spirit that flows from putting God first is recognised and ingrained with practice, religious practice. In a joke famous in the Jazz world a guy approaches a musician in the street in New York and asks: 'How do I get to Carnegie Hall?' The musician, a little ruefully, replies: 'You practise, man. You practise.'

None of this is to say that practice makes perfect. It is God who makes perfect. The free and undeserved gift of grace, the unconditional love of God in Christ for all, is the jewel hidden in the mud of the Christian church and in each of its broken and often deluded people. But if we are to live lives that give due thanks to God for the grace freely given, we may do so by practicing our religion, as indeed the Bible asks us over and over again to do.

On the way

In the Bible an early description of Christianity is 'The Way'.[4] The word is an ordinary one and it has escaped the fate of many Biblical words, the fate of becoming Christian jargon. It is still used in the Church today, though perhaps not often enough. So, for example, if you go as a seeker into Grace Cathedral, San Francisco, you will be invited to learn and put into effect '…a way of life that is spiritual, practical, reasonable, mystical and in service to the community and world.'

Here is a man, the early Quaker James Nayler, who saw the beauty of this way. In his troubled life he seems to have suffered serious mental illness and delusion, and therefore to be a poor witness in the court of critiquing. Nonetheless he drank true water from the underground stream, so that from his deathbed he could say:

> There is a spirit which I feel that delights to do no evil, nor to revenge any wrong, but delights to endure all things, in hope to enjoy its own in the end.
>
> Its hope is to outlive all wrath and contention, and to weary out all exaltation and cruelty, or whatever is of a nature contrary to itself.
>
> It sees to the end of all temptations. As it bears no evil in itself, so it conceives none in thought to any other.
>
> If it be betrayed, it bears it, for its ground and spring is the mercies and forgiveness of God. Its crown is meekness, its life is everlasting love unfeigned; it takes its kingdom with entreaty and not with contention, and keeps it by lowliness of mind.
>
> In God alone it can rejoice, though none else regard it, or can own its life. It is conceived in sorrow, and brought

forth without any to pity it; nor doth it murmur at grief and oppression.

It never rejoiceth but through sufferings; for with the world's joy it is murdered. I found it alone, being forsaken. I have fellowship therein with them who lived in dens and desolate places of the earth, who through death obtained this resurrection and eternal holy life.[5]

This is the way that overcomes all hatred. I hope that all God's people might face death with words and thoughts like this on their lips and in their hearts. Yet if we had been present at Nayler's deathbed to hear him we might have found his praise of quiet and indomitable love hard to understand, since his tongue had been burned through with a hot iron for saying the wrong things, and in looking at him we would have seen that his forehead bore the letter 'B', branded there to mark him as a blasphemer.

In the face of persecution, in the face of his own delusions and mental illness, this man seems to have understood the practice of his religion. It is by the late fruit of his prayers that he deserves now to be remembered.

'There is a spirit which I feel that delights to do no evil.' How may I come to die with the fortitude of James Nayler? Surely it is by coming to the moment of dependence on God, by living the faith in real time, by speaking out for those without a voice, in short by practising my religion; 'I felt you, and I knew you loved me'.[6]

In his book *Reimagining Christianity* Dean Alan Jones speaks of this:

> The way in which religion is usually presented misleads people into believing they cannot enter into a faith practice unless they wholeheartedly believe the doctrines of that faith. But to expect belief before doing the work is getting things backward. Patient practice, sometimes a lifetime's worth, is a prerequisite of true faith.[7]

Or as the Episcopal priest Broderick Greer has put it, on your bad days you just have to settle for being religious but not spiritual.

This makes sense to me. I was baptised as a child, and confirmed as a young adult in a ceremony that was emotionally deeply significant to me. And I gave my life to Christ in an intentional act of prayer and self-oblation on yet another day. But in the end I agree with Alan Jones that all these things in my life came to land because of practise. I'm a practising Christian, not only because I'm no expert and will never be one, but because only by practising can I live. Professor Martyn Percy in his excellent unfolding of Anglicanism speaks of the church as a 'community of practice' - 'groups of people who share a concern or passion for something they do and learn to do it better as they interact regularly'.[8]

Practice has about it, brings with it, a flexibility and a poetry and a beauty resilient enough to bear the stresses of experience, unlike the anxious and tense repetition of dogmatic truths, which for so many is just whistling in the dark, until some crisis comes and the carapace cracks, and another potential believer is lost to the family of faith.

In the Epistle of James we read this:

> True devotion, the kind that is pure and faultless before God the Father, is this: to care for orphans and widows in their difficulties and to keep the world from contaminating us.[9]

This is the description of a way of life and of a set of disciplines. It points to the inner and the outer journey. It speaks of justice for the poor and of holiness. It does not link these things conditionally to the grace of God. In short it offers a model for the shaping of the Christian life after the pattern of Christ, who restored to a widow her son alive, and who was tempted just as we are, yet without sin.

Nothing we can do will make God love us any more, nor any less. The practice of our religion teaches humility as well as holiness and justice, and may God help us if we believe that practice makes perfect.

All the same, light-hearted and gentle practice helps. Jascha Heifetz said of the violin: 'I have never believed in practising too much … never believed in grinding.' But he also said: 'If I don't practise one day, I know it; two days, the critics know it; three days, the public knows it.'

In speaking of practice I speak of words said and things done. I am not concerned here with the preferences of Christians as to how these words and things are to be spoken and said, nor of the relative value of some words and deeds against others. Too much ink, and not a little blood, has been spilled over all that as the years have passed. But to learn the language of the faith, and to become fluent in it, is constantly to speak the scripture and the creeds, and constantly to enact the liturgies of the Church. Later I shall I describe this speaking and doing as 'drinking from the fountain'.

Begin again

> Ever tried. Ever failed. No matter. Try again. Fail again. Fail better ... Try again. Fail again. Better again. Or better worse.[10]

Practice is not cumulative. There is no way to become 'advanced'. All we will ever be is increasingly experienced beginners.

It is as if we leave home each morning, determined to get that little bit closer to God whom we believe to be miles away, high in the mountains we can see far along the road. But each morning, to our distress, we find that we are stepping over the same threshold again. The journey never seems to get properly begun. No milestone ever seems to be reached. All we do is step out each day, our foot falling on the ground outside our own front door yet again. And slowly, imperceptibly, the threshold is worn away by the erosion of our daily practice. Until in the end we find to our astonishment that we have worn through, into the presence of God, who has always been there, not in the mountains miles away but undergirding our house, patiently waiting for the repetition of our beginnings to lead us to his waiting and everlasting arms.

Following the loving one

'In the evening of our life we will be examined in love', says John of the Cross, following St Paul in 1 Corinthians 13 – and in the evening of our life that examination will be the only one that matters. 'By this will all know that you are my disciples', says our Lord, 'if you have love for one another.' I do believe that disciplines of prayer, of evangelism and of service – in short of the practice of religion – are important here below; but their importance stops at the gate of heaven, where the eternal table is laid and the poor carpenter will sit, not beside us now but across from us, and he will look into our eyes, and love is all that will be measured there.

In the end practice, discipleship, is to be seen only in the light of love, and as a response to love, and as a manifestation of love. Disciples are simply learners gathered around a teacher at the table, or following a teacher on the road. The abiding image of discipleship for me is the sight of Jesus in Pier Paolo Pasolini's wonderful film *The Gospel According to St Matthew*, a movie dedicated to Pope John XXIII in which every word spoken is taken directly from scripture.

Pasolini was an outsider; a gay man, an atheist, a Marxist, who died by brutal violence. He was just the kind of person in fact with whom our Lord was wont to hang out in the Gospel according to St Matthew, as in all the gospels. In Pasolini's film the barefoot Jesus is seen tossing the words of the gospel over his shoulder, to his disciples, as they hurry along behind him, on the road. The words are caught by the wind, and Jesus himself is moving, moving, urgent, on the road. In this image the motivation for discipleship is not to amuse oneself or to earn a qualification. It is simply a readiness to run, to follow Jesus and to stay with Jesus, to hear those words and to be transformed by them, so that at the end of the day and the end of the road the disciples may meet at the table, and there perhaps ask him what he meant, just as his first disciples did.

I too would like to ask Jesus how best to follow him, just as my brothers and sisters did in the days of his life on earth. I believe that in the scriptures and the creeds, in the history of the Christian community, in the dialogue of prayer, his answer becomes plain – or rather, what becomes plain is what I must do, and continue to do, to receive the wisdom he will share.

In a religion built on grace, a discipleship that aims to mature and develop us is in one sense superfluous, and is certainly gratuitous. We are indeed taught in scripture to proclaim the mystery of Christ in us so as to present our friends to God as mature people,[11] and to run as an athlete runs who aims to win.[12] But we follow our Lord who has already given us the gift of life. And if we follow in the spirit of the One we follow, who was anointed with the oil of gladness beyond all his companions[13] then we follow playfully and joyously. We do not overlook that his road leads to, and through, the cross. Nor do we refuse to take up our own cross on that road as he asks. But we can be content on that road to be thankful and to rest as we enter his rest, since we follow the One whose yoke is easy and whose burden is light.[14]

For me, reflecting on that serious and playful road, four dimensions of Christian practice have come into focus. They are to meet at the table (which is the essence and the foundation), and there to drink from the fountain, and there to watch in the moment, and from there to stretch for the kingdom. I'll spend much of the rest of this book trying to show what I mean by these.

Part II

5. Meeting at the table

Friends of God

This is my commandment: love each other just as I have loved you. No one has greater love than to give up one's life for one's friends. You are my friends if you do what I command you. I don't call you servants any longer, because servants don't know what their master is doing. Instead, I call you friends, because everything I heard from my Father I have made known to you. You didn't choose me, but I chose you and appointed you so that you could go and produce fruit and so that your fruit could last. As a result, whatever you ask the Father in my name, he will give you. I give you these commandments so that you can love each other.[1]

To be, not just seem to be, a friend of God.[2]

In my inaugural sermon I said: *'It's a table like a table at a wedding. You sit with guests you never knew, and you find out about them, and they become your friends.'*

Meeting at that table is the foundation of the Christian life. The poor carpenter Jesus made and laid the table as his Father wished, for his friends. We sit close beside him there. As we do so, reading and remembering the stories about him in God's word, we remember his commitment to his friends. I do believe that when we do what he commands us we are his friends indeed, we are the ones for whom with the greatest love he laid down his life.

So we look in the same direction with him, at one another and at the empty seats around the table. Those seats are reserved for people not yet present, and we look beyond the table at the streets and homes of the ones who might sit with us one day, and we commit ourselves to meet them, too.

A friend of mine

Why do people say 'a friend of mine'? You never hear anyone say, 'Oh, Andy Rackstraw is a very good plumber of mine.' 'Dr Jones, an excellent anaesthetist of mine'. 'Justin Welby, the Archbishop of mine'.

When we are talking about friends, we ourselves are central to the picture. The word 'friend' is relational in a very strong way. No one is a friend in the abstract. If I simply say 'Alice is a friend', you will automatically think that she is a friend *of mine*. I am claiming Alice. If you know Alice and I claim her as a friend, then I am telling you something about myself. I am committing myself.

Friendship commits. It is powerful and not easily broken. 'Rackstraw was my plumber, but he specialises in lead pipe-work now.' 'Jones was my anaesthetist, but now she's on maternity leave.' 'Welby was my Archbishop, but now I live in Scotland.' No one is demeaned or threatened by these changes. But what about 'You used to be a friend of mine, but not any more'? This says something very personal about you, and about me, and about our future.

Carpenters make tables. Lovers make love. What do friends make? Well, nothing. They make friends. Friendship commits and binds, but as we sit at the table together our relationship is also gratuitous, playful, unproductive. It is an end, not a means. Playful as it is, it is a matter of life and death, because it is a matter of love. St John says:

> We know that we have transferred from death to life, because we love the brothers and sisters. The person who does not love remains in death.[3]

Friendship commits, and it commits you to tell the truth, as you sit at the square table of the carpenter, looking into the eyes of your friend opposite. Jesus told us that we would know the truth, and that the truth would set us free. And so as friends we commit to people as they are, not as they pretend to be.

Friendship commits, and the richest friendships commit you to a group. One-to-one friendship is a precious thing, but as C. S. Lewis pointed out, group friendship is even more rich:

> In each of my friends there is something that only some other friend can fully bring out. By myself I am not large enough to call the whole man into activity ... Now that Charles is dead, I shall never again see Ronald's reaction to a specifically Caroline joke. Far from having more of Ronald, having him 'to myself' now that Charles is away, I have less of Ronald.

Hence, true Friendship is the least jealous of loves … In this, Friendship exhibits a glorious 'nearness by resemblance' to Heaven itself where the very multitude of the blessed … increases the fruition which each has of God.[4]

In this illustration Lewis draws on his own life. 'Charles' is Charles Williams, and 'Ronald' is J. R(onald) R. Tolkien. Their friendship was expressed in their weekly commitment to one another, every Thursday evening, in the life of the Inklings. Friendship flowed into, informed and shaped their creative writing. Even when they disagreed, their friendship committed them. Tolkien said of Lewis, 'His greatest gift to me was sheer encouragement'.[5] Through the friendship of the Inklings, an enormous richness was released into the world. Lewis's words on the unselfishness of friendship were truer than even he knew.

Friendship commits, and this can be problematic. We worry if our children choose their friends poorly, although when we talk about this, we usually avoid the word 'friendship'. Perhaps we don't want to spoil the word. So we say 'She's got in with the wrong crowd'. 'He's in bad company.' Meanwhile if our own friends turn out to be difficult people, then we have a problem, because we are committed.

So friendship is intimate, powerful, far-reaching. It involves me, my claims and my commitments.

And yet in another sense it seems to have nothing to do with me. At the carpenter's table I sit beside a rag-tag crew whom I did not choose, and who seem to have very little in common. It seems that friendship too is a mystery, a mystery bearing a hope.

In a few pages' time I will talk about the group of friends round Jesus' table in the days of his incarnate life. They model the group of friends who sit there today. It's evident from the Gospels that in itself this group of friends was neither homogenous nor harmonious. They were socially and politically extremely disparate. They jockeyed for position, and they and their mothers argued about who should be first. Knowing all this Jesus still said 'You are friends of mine'. Being at the table was not in the end their choice. They did not choose him, but he chose them.

It seems they were only friends at all insofar as they were friends of his. Their choice boiled down to this; would they accept his choice? Chosen to be his friends, putting their choice with his choice, they then had no choice over his other friends. Any friend of Jesus was to be – by definition – a friend of theirs.

There is a dining table, the long table, in the British House of Lords. There the rule is that you sit at the next available seat and you connect with those already sitting there and those who come to sit beside you next, whether you know them or not, whether you like them or not. As one of the Lords has said: 'You plonk yourself next to whoever and the significance of that is that you often find yourself sitting next to somebody who is not necessarily from the same party.' In the echo-chamber world of exclusive friendships, in the world of social media and social silos, the long table speaks of dialogue beyond choosing. In doing so it speaks of the table of the poor Christ, which has always been like that, whenever it has been faithful to the One who made it.

In the House of Lords you can walk away from the table after the meal if the conversation has gone poorly. At the carpenter's table things are more permanent. You're stuck with the people there, for as long as they or you choose to stay there. The friendship to which Jesus calls, friendship beyond choice and beyond liking, can be hard, and the many divisions of the church through the ages underline how hard it can be. But in the strength of the table's builder and host it is possible to sit and stay – possible for anyone.

Of course Jesus also told us to love our enemies. But as Sallie McFague has said, 'In Hebrew thought the opposite of friend is not enemy but stranger'.[6] You might think that our enemies by definition are those who are not at the table with us, and of course there are many who want a table where no one disagrees. And indeed raised voices at the table, and the sharing of hard truths there, can make sitting with friends a very uncomfortable experience.

But it is only as friendship grows, and trust grows, that honesty too can flourish. Whenever I have made mildly controversial statements in the church and beyond it, a good many critical and abusive statements have come my way, almost all via social media, anonymous or at best remote. But now and again a few people have been prepared to sit with me so as to be truthful, so that we might speak and listen together. I honour them for their commitment. I hope conversations like that will continue.

In the book of Proverbs we are told, 'Faithful are the wounds of a friend; but the kisses of an enemy are deceitful'.[7] When the General Synod of the Church of England engaged in its process of 'shared conversation' around human sexuality, the process was not emotionally easy, and the practical outcomes were inevitably inconclusive. But the response of Synod members to the process itself, to the discipline of sitting in small groups at a table and of speaking the truth in love, was almost universally positive. And the question was raised by many there, 'How can we continue down this road of meeting? How can we keep talking and listening honestly?' It was a very good question. They were asking for a table.

At my wedding service in 1976, Kate and I included an additional reading; a selection of phrases from the Jewish philosopher Martin Buber, whose writings among other things had led me to Christ. The reading contained one of Buber's most famous phrases, 'All real living is meeting'. It continued with words still more profound for me: 'Feelings dwell in people, but people dwell in their love'.[8] In asking for these words at our wedding we wanted to remember where love rests, and where love begins and ends, and whose love it is.

People fall in love, romantically, and then one of two things happens. Either they fall out of love, or they stop falling but stay in love: they stand in love. Marriage works when people stand in love. Friendship, too, works when people stand in it. The emotions that come with friendship are not central to it.

None of this is to take away from the marvellous experience of long and close personal friendship with one or two people, that so many of us value and treasure. It is a great gift to be with like-minded people, with soul-mates. But at the carpenter's table we are called to lay another and equally precious understanding alongside it; friendship with the ones called alongside us, for reasons we do not know. These things are both rightly called by the same name; friendship. They belong on the same shelf, in the same bag together.

In 1145 the monk Aelred became Abbot of Rievaulx, miles from anywhere in Yorkshire. There he wrote his book of dialogues on

Christian Friendship, the first and still the greatest reflection on the subject from within the Christian Church.

Aelred's friendships there were restricted to the other monks, and he did not choose the friends he had. His is therefore not a romantic book:

> *Walter:* Unless we are greatly mistaken, you used to be friendly with an irascible man. We have heard it said that he often injured you, and yet, to the day of his death, you never said an unkind word against him. *Aelred:* Some people are by nature irascible ... If we make friends with such people, we must bear patiently with them.[9]

And yet for Aelred, hanging out with the irascible or the mistaken or the annoying was a calling, and it led to a reward. 'Friendship is agreement on things sacred and profane, accompanied by goodwill and love'[10]. He valued it.

C. S. Lewis could see Aelred's point, and he saw himself in the same tradition. He valued friendship too, but he believed that he was in a dwindling minority:

> ...very few modern people think Friendship a love of comparable value [to affection, or erotic love], or even a love at all ... To the Ancients, Friendship seemed the happiest and most human of all loves; the crown of love and the school of virtue. The modern world, in comparison, ignores it ... it is something quite marginal; not a main course in life's banquet; a diversion; something that fills up the chinks of one's time.[11]

It is in this context – of friendship as a choice, and of a society which values it oddly – that the Christian community has chosen to be around a table and to be friendly there.

Friendship as I'm using it here is not a common word in church circles. Instead Christians have preferred to talk of 'fellowship'. This word in our English Bibles almost always translates the Greek word *koinonia.* But in today's Church 'fellowship' has become a poor word for several reasons.

The Biblical *koinonia* is very rich. Sometimes it means 'community'. Sometimes it means 'friendship'. Sometimes it means 'partnership'. In 1 Corinthians Paul uses it to refer to the financial collection for the poor in Jerusalem – a concrete piece of love. 'Fellowship' is a pastel-coloured word compared to all this.

Another thing; today we are rightly sensitive to gender in language. 'Fellowship' implies a group of men, good fellows together, hail-fellow-well-met. This may be the way to see the all-male Fellowship of the Ring, but it will not do for the Church. And the phrase 'Ladies' Fellowship' just goes to show that two wrongs don't make a right.

Some churches use it as another word for 'congregation' – 'Our fellowship meets on Sundays at 10.00 a.m.'. This begs far too many questions about the relationship between what Jesus did with his group and what we do on Sunday mornings.

Finally, like many words used by the Christian community, 'fellowship' has lost any common meaning in the world beyond the church. It has become a Christian jargon word, meaning different things to different Christians, but not meaning much at all outside the Christian subculture .

For these reasons I won't be using it here. Instead I will stick with 'friendship' and 'friendliness'. To do so, to see the table as a place for friends, is increasingly a prophetic act.

Prophetic friendliness

Our society is becoming radically privatised and fragmented, but not everyone sees that as a problem. The self-sufficient and the wealthy in particular tend not to mind it.

When the sharing of the peace was introduced into the Eucharist, it quickly became a bone of contention. It was seen as a physical symptom of a church that was looking too hard for friendship. A coalition grew to oppose it. This had various strands. They included emotionally inhibited Englishmen and Englishwomen ('Have we been introduced?') and those whose theology had no room for the human community ('It's just me and my Maker, Vicar!').

Together with these were people who were afraid that a cheap togetherness would devalue the Faith:

> In a sense, the more shy and retiring we are, the better. Nothing is more tiresome than the gregarious young priest

who overwhelms his parishioners with 'friendship', slaps
people on the back and asks them to call him 'Tom'…[12]

Indeed that gregarious young priest became a stock comedy
character, and he has remained one for over forty years. He took
over this comic role from Alan Bennett's clergyman, who, goodness
knows, is still recognisable enough:

> Some of us think life's a bit like that, don't we? But it isn't.
> Life, you know, is rather like opening a tin of sardines. We all
> of us are looking for the key. And I wonder how many of you
> here tonight have wasted years of your lives looking behind
> the kitchen dressers of this life for that key. I know I have.
> Others think they've found the key, don't they? They roll back
> the lid of the sardine tin of life. They reveal the sardines—the
> riches of life—therein, and they get them out, and they enjoy
> them. But, you know, there's always a little bit in the corner
> you can't get out. I wonder is there a little bit in the corner
> of your life? I know there is in mine![13]

If you can bear to laugh at something so accurate, it will be because
you know that Bennett's pompous ass is living in a world of his own.
In contrast what is funny about 'Tom' seems to be that he wants to
live in our world – to be friendly. According to his amused or angry
critics, poor 'Tom' has missed the point. Doesn't he know (they say)
that it is precisely aloneness, or aloofness, that distant sort of mystery,
that draws his parishioners to church in the first place?

Even preferment does not get 'Tom' off the hook. Many years
ago Monica Furlong grumbled about:

> … a habit of speaking about a bishop in conversation by his
> title and Christian name – Bishop Tom, Bishop Jim, Bishop
> Tim … I fear what it indicates is a willed intimacy, a pretence
> that bishop, clergy and laity are on much closer terms than
> they actually are. It is not very convincing.[14]

Most of those who laugh at 'Tom' or 'Bishop Tom' would not see
themselves as members of the Christian community. But if these
scoffers ever do go to church it is not for friendship. They will find
that elsewhere, if they seek it at all.

So to the 'cultured despisers', our faith has become a source of mockery precisely when it acts like people round a table; in other words at the point of friendship and community. Their toes curl at the very thought of sharing the peace, being friendly, smiling. These things are right up there with strumming guitars, waving tambourines and the Alpha course, on the naughty shelf of the fastidious, for whom they are seen as sharp indicators that the church has lost its way.

With unusual fortitude and consistency, in the teeth of all this opposition from the socially comfortable (or from those so deeply wounded that they no longer feel their loneliness), the people of Jesus Christ have continued to sit around his table, and to be friendly there. It has been a most unpopular choice.

Very little has annoyed the cultured world so much as the church's cheerful commitment to friendliness. Disdainful laughter reaches to the skies. As a parish priest I heard echoes of it every time I asked on Sundays who had had a birthday, and every time our community sang 'Happy Birthday' to them (it happened about four weeks out of five).

Against all this exalted mockery, at the carpenter's table, there sits the local church. Frankly, it is usually an odd bunch.

In my experience in England today, the people's table will contain disproportionate numbers of the lonely, the elderly ('When someone shakes my hand at church, it's the only time in the week anyone touches me'), single parents, younger children, those with a learning disability, and those who choose to sit there not because it is cosy, but because Jesus promised that he would be found there too.

The friendliness of the local church is a prophetic act, valued most by those who need it most. Like all prophecy, the friendliness of the church confronts. It demands a decision. Will you sit at the long table? Will you look in the same direction as the carpenter who invited you? Will you identify with the flotsam of the community and get to know the people you would never otherwise know, or want to know?

'Such a friendly church'. Despite all the grumpiness I have mentioned, when you hear this inside a church building it is not usually said as an insult, but a compliment. It does not simply mean that the church is full of people who are friends of one another. If you are new, that can be the mark of a most *un*friendly church. For a stranger to describe a community as friendly means that friendship has been offered, openly. And when it is openly offered, friendship is recognised for what it is. It is not normally refused.

Open friendship

> John the Baptist came neither eating bread nor drinking wine, and you say, 'He has a demon.' Yet the Human One[16] came eating and drinking, and you say, 'Look, a glutton and a drunk, a friend of tax collectors and sinners.' But wisdom is proved to be right by all her descendants.[17]

Winston Churchill liked pigs. When asked why, he replied, 'Cats look down on you as your superiors. Dogs look up to you like your servants. But a pig will treat you as an equal'.

The outstanding German theologian Jürgen Moltmann would have seen the point of this:

> One does not have to submit to a friend. One neither looks up to nor down at a friend. One can look a friend in the face.[18]

Alongside this natural and satisfying equality, Moltmann speaks about the world-changing act of Jesus in making his table open to all, thus shattering the exclusive peer group.

> The closed circle of friendship among peers is broken in principle by Christ, not only in relation to the bad humanity of 'despised' society, but in relation to God. Had he abided by the peer principle, he would of necessity have had to stay in heaven … For this reason Christian friendship also cannot be lived within a closed circle of the faithful and the pious, of peers in other words, but only in open affection and public respect of others.[19]

Moltmann coined the phrase 'open friendship' to describe the church's way of relating. For him friendship is the right word to describe Jesus' relationship with us because it is so unpretentious.

'Friend' is 'not a functional title, nor a designation of office, nor a role one is expected to play in society.[20]

If friendship is not these things, what is it?

It is a personal relation, 'someone who likes you', someone you like.[21]

The friendship we are talking about here is not to be faked, and indeed it cannot be. Politicians and chat-show hosts attempt to do so all the time, to their own loss. For Moltmann 'friends open up to one another free space for free life'[22]. He sees friendship as a relationship free of power-games (though not free of the truth of power). As such it is the natural mark of the table-community of Jesus, who said that we were to know the truth, and that the truth would set us free. In English, as in Moltmann's German, the word 'friend' is rooted in older words which mean 'free one'.

Friendship can take power and turn it into freedom. For example parents are responsible for their children until the children come of age. Then there is the chance for us to enter a new relationship with our children, the relationship of friends at the table by choice together. I say the chance. It is not automatic, and it cannot be. In the case of each child, friendship is a possibility that depends on freedom. But the most priceless gift an adult child can give a parent is to admit them to the company of their friendship.

This can also be true, says Moltmann, for other power-relationships in society – black/white, master/servant, man/woman.

There is neither Jew nor Greek; there is neither slave nor free; nor is there male and female, for you are all one in Christ Jesus.[23]

If we are indeed one, what is our relationship at the table to be? Friendship. 'The friend is the new person, the true person, the free person, the person who likes to be with other people.'[24]

Finally, Moltmann sketches what a church of friendship would look like:

What would it be like if Christian congregations and communities were no longer to regard themselves only as 'the community of saints' or as 'the congregation of the faithful' but as such a 'community of friends'? ... Then they would have to assemble in grass roots communities that would live close to the people and with the people in the friendship of Jesus.[25]

The thinking of this German Protestant is echoed by an Italian Roman Catholic. Carlo Carretto contributed significantly to the life of the Church in Italy as youth director of Catholic Action. Discontented with the association of many in the church with the political right, and moved to connect more with God in prayer, he joined the Little Brothers of Jesus in 1954. Carretto has been described as 'basically simple and poor, gifted and flawed and surely firmer in his faith than are most of us'. [26]

Writing for the Roman Catholic church in the early1980s, he sought to defend the extraordinary flowering of movements and apostolates there – Catholic Action, the Focolare, etc. He had to defend them because they were being attacked in the Roman Catholic family, sometimes for reasons which will now be familiar ('The Focolarini smile too much').[27]

And in a lyrical and prophetic passage which has motivated my own ministry ever since I first read it thirty years ago, he points to the church of the underground stream, the church of wonder and hope:

> Today's people...want a Church made of friendship, of genuine contacts, of mutual interchange of little things. But more than anything else, a Church that feeds them with the Word, a Church that works with them by physically taking them by the hand, a Church whose face is like that of the Church of Luke, of Mark, of John, a Church that is just starting – that smells of beginnings.[28]

'A church that is just starting'... Carretto is thinking of Jesus' own group.

Jesus' group in Jesus' time

> Jesus said: I am the Shepherd, the Beautiful One, and I know mine and mine know me, and just in that way the Father knows me and I know the Father, and I lay my life down for the sheep.[1]

None of this talk of tables and Christian friendship would mean much unless you can see it in the incarnate life of the Son of God. What did Jesus do?

Jesus in relationship

For Christians Jesus is the Son of God, one person of three in the eternal and undivided Trinity, the unbounded community of love. The doctrine of the Trinity is a picture drawn around a mystery. No one has ever seen God, but with confidence we can say that we believe the life of the Godhead is relational life. And within that relational life, by God's own choice, '...the Word became flesh and lived among *us*.'[2] In the days of his human life on earth Jesus did not sit at the table alone.

He was born and grew to manhood in the community of a family in a village. He travelled to Jerusalem as one of a group of travellers, and visited the temple there as a boy so that he could be in the midst of a group of teachers.

He stood in the midst of John's community at his baptism. He was transfigured in the presence of three of his friends. He sat with his group at the table on the night before he died. He was crucified as one of three criminals. At the foot of his cross stood the distressed fragments of his community. A group of people cared for his body after his death.

After his resurrection he walked to Emmaus as one of three. In the upper room he breathed his Spirit on his group. At the lakeside he prepared breakfast for his friends. On the mountain, while he was giving the group his blessing, he parted from them.

And for three and a half years he engaged in his ministry.

Inviting to the table

> I assure you that we speak about what we know and testify about what we have seen ...[3]

Jesus' ministry was full of variety, incident, glory and trouble. He preached publicly to thousands and fed them. He ministered God's healing to all those who asked him, and a few more besides. He and his disciples wore themselves out in the pastoral care of the crowds.

He also spent a great deal of time alone with his Father, awake and waiting in the moments of stillness.

But the Gospels show one overwhelming priority. They say that the main thing Jesus did with his time was to choose a small group of people and to sit with them, to spend time with them. Almost exactly half of St Mark's Gospel is devoted to time spent by Jesus with the disciples.[4]

The word 'invest' has come to have a mainly financial meaning but it comes from the Latin investire, 'to put on clothes'. To invest your life in someone is to give them your life, so that they can put it on like a coat.

> Jesus went up on a mountain and called those he wanted, and they came to him. He appointed twelve and called them apostles. He appointed them to be with him, to be sent out to preach, and to have authority to throw out demons.[5]

Jesus invested his life in his group. From among them he chose twelve – twelve, to say something symbolic about Israel. But these twelve were not headhunted to do a job. Eventually they were indeed sent out, which is what 'apostles' means, to proclaim the message and to stretch for the kingdom. But the first reason Jesus chose them was 'to be with him'.

With him, and with others, they lived a travelling life. Their table was a borrowed table, since he had nowhere to lay his head. Or you might say it was a campaign table, erected and dismantled each day. This way of living automatically produces honesty – more honesty than you might want, as anyone who has been on even the briefest residential or holiday with a group will know.

Jesus' group was not only the twelve but included many others, primarily the 'fascinating network of women', and others again; for example Lazarus, for example Joseph of Arimathea. The apostles themselves did not think they were special in this sense. They were clear that others had shared their lives in full:

> During this time, the family of believers was a company of about one hundred and twenty persons. Peter stood among them and said: 'Friends ... we must select one of those who have accompanied us during the whole time the Lord Jesus

> lived among us, beginning from the baptism of John until the day when Jesus was taken from us. This person must become along with us a witness to his resurrection.' So they nominated two: Joseph called Barsabbas, who was also known as Justus, and Matthias ....[6]

This was their life; table life. They had what 'the crowds' by definition never had. For them the experience of Jesus was a face to face, small-group experience. These people were given the priceless gift of human time, what we now call 'quality time', with the incarnate Lord. He really was at the table with them – not at the high table in the same room, but at their own table, beside them.

To Nicodemus Jesus said 'We speak of what we know ...'[7]. At his baptism he identified himself with John and with those who came to John. Then, having called his group to the table, he identifies himself with them. Their teaching comes from Jesus alone; but their testimony is what they know *together*.

So the priority of Jesus' ministry, and the context of Jesus' teaching, is the common life of a group. It is not exclusive; over and over again its doors are opened to others. *It is not exclusive.* There is no qualification for entry other than the act of entry itself. But it is not cheap. So when its door is opened to others, they do not always step in:

> When Jesus heard this, he said, 'There's one more thing. Sell everything you own and distribute the money to the poor. Then you will have treasure in heaven. And come, follow me.' When he heard these words, the man became sad because he was extremely rich.[8]

The group was not unusual. It was based on a commonly available model, as the church always is. Many such groups existed in its day, itinerant groups of teachers and their followers.

What happened in this group? Life happened. The life of the disciples, their meals at table, their jealousies and squabbles, their parties, their travels, their worries about sick relatives, their work, their shared hopes, the demands made on them. This life was not church life, not 'spiritual life'. It was their common life. Although the disciples asked Jesus to teach them to pray, there is no evidence that they constituted a prayer group. Their life was meat and potatoes, daily bread, not a worship service, not sherry (or coffee, or doughnuts) after such a service.

And Jesus invested his life in all of this. The shared life became the medium of the Gospel message. From the very beginning it was as Lesslie Newbigin said, 'The only [thing that communicates] the gospel is a community that lives by it.'[9] Adolf Harnack made the same point over a century ago: 'It was community (*koinonia*), and not any evangelist, which proved to be the most effective missionary.'[10]

Extending the group

> We announce to you what existed from the beginning, what we have heard, what we have seen with our eyes, what we have seen and our hands handled, about the word of life. The life was revealed, and we have seen, and we testify and announce to you the eternal life that was with the Father and was revealed to us. What we have seen and heard, we also announce it to you so that you can have *koinonia* with us. Our *koinonia* is with the Father and with his Son, Jesus Christ.[11]

These are the opening words of 1 John. The writer is aiming at Christians, some time after the Crucifixion/Resurrection of Jesus. He wants to combat false teaching in their church.

He needs to authenticate himself. He can find no better way to do this than to say that he has been at the table, in the group, with Jesus.

He is a teacher. He teaches as an individual – 'I am writing to you…'. But he testifies in the plural – 'we declare to you …', 'we have seen …' – as a member of Jesus' group.

He wants to combat false teaching, but his recipe for holding a church fast to the truth does not begin with teaching at all. He begins by remembering the group, the relationship.

What is John remembering?

He remembers that Jesus laid bare what was in his, John's, heart. But he also saw what was in Jesus' heart. He saw him strong, fresh, loving; he saw him hungry, angry, lonely, tired, and near the end he saw him in despair. He saw Jesus in the setting of his group.

At the heart of Christian life is a mystery and a hope. The mystery comes true for John, and the hope can be grasped, when he talks about extending this relationship to the community of his readers.

> ... so that you can have *koinonia* with us. Our *koinonia* is with the Father and with his Son, Jesus Christ.

John believes that the relationship of the group is not simply *imitated* in the church that receives his letter. He believes it is *extended*.[12] Believing that this extension is possible, he points us back to what Jesus thought was possible.

> I'm not praying only for them but also for those who believe in me because of their word. I pray they will be one, Father, just as you are in me and I am in you. I pray that they also will be in us, so that the world will believe that you sent me. I've given them the glory that you gave me so that they can be one just as we are one. I'm in them and you are in me so that they will be made perfectly one. Then the world will know that you sent me and that you have loved them just as you loved me.[13]

The ecumenical movement has been rightly inspired by these words. But Jesus was not talking here about the formal unity of organisations, but about the extension of his group's life; the extension of the table of companions.

All four gospels agree. At the beginning of his ministry, after his temptation, Jesus did three things: he preached, he healed and he chose a group. The reign of God was manifest in all three. Of the three, the group was the foundation. In Matthew, Mark and John stories of the founding of the community come explicitly before the first miracle of healing. In Luke, Jesus' relationship with Simon has been established before his first miracle is done.[14] The Kingdom of God is wherever God is King. Jesus' ministry flowed, and still flows, from the life of his group. And the group's life was lived, and is still lived, in the spirit of Jesus.

St Paul and Jesus' group

Anyone who takes the Bible seriously, and who wants to see group life as important, must come to grips with St Paul. On the face of it, it would be difficult to imagine a less group-minded spirit. Surely Paul is the patron saint of loners?

Flying solo

In the world's faith communities most people think that we meet God best when we are by ourselves.

Plotinus thought so, and he said 'life is the flight of the alone to the Alone'. Kierkegaard was one of many individuals who agreed with him and followed this route.

There are those in every community, however committed it is to group life, who are not joiners. And the truth is that most church communities are not, in fact, committed to group life.

Because natural religion tends to solitude, seeing Christian life as an extendable table, extending the life of Jesus' group, has been a minority pursuit in church history. People have seen it as a counsel of perfection (okay for monks and nuns, or for the ones Kipling's character calls 'holy-bolies') or as a consumer choice (okay for extraverts and those who like that sort of thing). Those who see things this way may well be cheered to think that they have St Paul on their side. But are they right?

Paul as mystic and maverick

St Paul experienced mystical revelation on his own:

> I know a man in Christ who was caught up into the third heaven fourteen years ago. I don't know whether it was in the body or out of the body. God knows. I know that this man was caught up into paradise and that he heard unspeakable words that were things no one is allowed to repeat.[15]

He came to terms with his experience of conversion by himself:

> But God had set me apart from birth and called me through his grace. He was pleased to reveal his Son to me, so that I might preach about him to the Gentiles. I didn't immediately

consult with any human being. I didn't go up to Jerusalem to see the men who were apostles before me either, but I went away into Arabia...[16]

Paul found it hard sometimes to sit at the table. He fell out with colleagues:

Some time later, Paul said to Barnabas, 'Let's go back and visit all the brothers and sisters in every city where we preached the Lord's word. Let's see how they are doing.' Barnabas wanted to take John Mark with them. Paul insisted that they shouldn't take him along, since he had deserted them in Pamphylia and hadn't continued with them in their work. Their argument became so intense that they went their separate ways. Barnabas took Mark and sailed to Cyprus. Paul chose Silas and left...[17]

He was seen as a loose cannon by earlier members of Jesus' group. The writer of 2 Peter says:

... just as our dear friend and brother Paul wrote to you according to the wisdom given to him, speaking of these things in all his letters. Some of his remarks are hard to understand, and people who are ignorant and whose faith is weak twist them to their own destruction, just as they do the other scriptures.[18]

In wanting to be alone, he is of course not alone. It is perfectly possible to live a form of the Christian life without the sort of small-group commitments that I am imagining when I speak of sitting at the table. Very many Christians do. But I think they would be mistaken if they tried to claim St Paul too enthusiastically as their model.

Paul in Jesus' group

From the moment Ananias prayed for him that he might receive his sight, 'Brother Saul' was a member of Jesus' extended group.

Ananias went to the house. He placed his hands on Saul and said, 'Brother Saul, the Lord sent me – Jesus, who appeared to you on the way as you were coming here. He sent me so that you could see again and be filled with the Holy Spirit.'

Instantly, flakes fell from Saul's eyes and he could see again. He got up and was baptized. After eating, he regained his strength. He stayed with the disciples in Damascus for several days … When Saul arrived in Jerusalem, he tried to join the disciples …[19]

After his controversy with Barnabas over John Mark, Paul did not give up on people. He immediately replaced Barnabas with Silas, later adding Timothy, and of course Luke himself. These were intimate travelling companions, companions at the table, not fellow eight-o-clockers dimly spotted across a deserted church. When Paul journeyed in Acts, he travelled with his group, that is with Jesus' extended group. From his own writings we know that he found it hard to minister without the support of his companions:

When I came to Troas to preach Christ's gospel, the Lord gave me an opportunity to preach. *But I was worried because I couldn't find my brother Titus there.* So I said good-bye to them and went on to Macedonia.[20]

There is only one record in Acts of Paul explicitly alone, and we can see there how he felt about it. In Acts 17, after some trouble in Beroea, we read that

… The brothers and sisters sent Paul away to the seacoast at once, but Silas and Timothy remained at Beroea. Those who escorted Paul led him as far as Athens, then returned *with instructions for Silas and Timothy to come to him as quickly as possible.*[21]

While he was waiting in Athens he preached, controversially as usual:

Some people joined him and came to believe…[22]

What did they join? There was no structure, but only Paul. They joined him at the carpenter's table; they shared his life, and the life of Christ made visible in community.

Paul's companions in ministry are commonly referred to today as a 'team'. This implies a group of working colleagues. But living the life of a travelling group in a hostile environment was an intense matter. The dynamic was the same for Paul as it was for Jesus.

And in the time he spent in the towns of his mission, he built relationships. An example of the quality of these relationships can be seen at Miletus, where Paul bids farewell to the Ephesian elders:

> After he said these things, he knelt down with all of them to pray. They cried uncontrollably as everyone embraced and kissed Paul. They were especially grieved by his statement that they would never see him again.[23]

And our final view of Paul in Acts is of him in Rome, where

> Paul lived in his own rented quarters for two full years and welcomed everyone who came to see him. Unhindered and with complete confidence, he continued to preach God's kingdom and to teach about the Lord Jesus Christ.[24]

The image is not of a man running a private night-school, but of one extending hospitality as the vessel of his teaching. The welcome comes first.

Paul was crusty, complicated – as we all are, or perhaps in his case more so. He knew the Lord in his own prayer and in silence and in solitude, waiting in the moment, as Jesus knew his Father, as we all should know God as part of our discipleship. But the royal road for him was as a member of Jesus' group. Where he could not find it, he built it.

And Paul inhabited, and inherited, and offered what he knew. It was the table of the forsaken and risen carpenter, the table of one he persecuted, the table of the one who forgave him and invited him to sit and eat. We have it still.

Jesus' group today

> From Paul, a slave of Christ Jesus … To those in Rome who are dearly loved by God and called to be God's people. Grace to you and peace from God our Father and the Lord Jesus Christ … I'll visit you when I go to Spain. I hope to see you while I'm passing through. And I hope you will send me on my way

there, after I have first been reenergized by some time in your
company.[1]

It is better to be bothered about quality rather than
quantity: a tiny diamond is far more valuable than a lorry-load
of stones. It is for that reason that we are going to work with
groups and small communities rather than large crowds … A
spoonful of sugar dissolved in a small cup sweetens the coffee,
and that is the way with the Gospel in a small community.[2]
I have spoken in faith of sitting beside the poor carpenter at
his table, looking his way, and seeing what he sees. The voice
of faith is bold – it says that we, who are His body, are indeed
seeing through his eyes.

But this is not the same as seeing him with our own eyes. Jesus
is ascended. The years of his earthly ministry are over. Two thousand
years later we can't help but be envious of those first disciples,
who knew Jesus in the flesh. Surely, they had a special deal. If only
we had been there, would it not have been easier to follow Jesus
than it often seems to be now? We know that we have to walk by
faith, not by sight, and despite what Jesus said to Thomas, we can
feel disadvantaged. And yet Jesus' words to Thomas, as John reports
them, are so clear.

> After eight days his disciples were again in a house and Thomas
> was with them. Even though the doors were locked, Jesus
> entered and stood among them. He said, 'Peace be with you.'
> Then he said to Thomas, 'Put your finger here. Look at my
> hands. Put your hand into my side. No more disbelief. Believe!'
> Thomas responded to Jesus, 'My Lord and my God!'
> Jesus replied, 'Do you believe because you see me?
> Happy are those who don't see and yet believe.'
> Then Jesus did many other miraculous signs in his disciples'
> presence, signs that aren't recorded in this scroll. But these
> things are written so that you will believe that Jesus is the
> Christ, God's Son, and that believing, you will have life in
> his name.[3]

'Blessed are those who have not seen'. Yet in the very next verse, John talks about even more that he himself has seen, with his eyes. Easy for him to say, then.

And yet the challenge and the extraordinary claim of those who sit at the carpenter's table is that we are in the same situation as John, and Mary and Salome and Peter. As Graham Pulkingham has said: 'The same dynamic that Jesus gave his disciples by his physical presence in his earthly ministry – *exactly this same dynamic* – is available to us by his Spirit' in the Church today.[4]

Even as we say it, these words may well make us blink. Have we – has Pulkingham – looked at the church today?

A tailor is asked to make a pair of trousers. He takes a whole month to do so. The irate client refuses to pay. 'After all', he says, 'God only took seven days to make the whole world!' The argument does not impress the tailor. 'Yes', he replies, 'but look at the world. And – look at these trousers!'

Look at the church. And look at this claim!

But Pulkingham is right. The dynamic he is pointing to can be available wherever Jesus is recognised, by two or three gathered together at his table.

Professor David Ford has called it 'a community of the face'.[5] Living in Jesus' group does not depend on any particular outward form – though it always helps to learn from tried and tested forms. It doesn't need a monastic community, nor the kind of charismatic residential community that Graham Pulkingham lived in, nor a nuclear family. It doesn't need a grant from the Church Commissioners. It doesn't depend on a particular institutional shape in the wider church. You don't actually even need a table! It looks different in every time and in every place.

And yet I think there is a necessary minimum. Wherever this is present, the face of Christ can be seen in the community of the face, around the table, around the group. That necessary minimum is simply this: *two, three or more Christians meeting one another with a durable honesty, so that they know life-changing friendship leading to repentance and ministry.* Let's look at these phrases in more detail.

'Two, three or more Christians ...'

> 'Again I assure you that if two of you agree on earth
> about anything you ask, then my Father who is in
> heaven will do it for you. For where two or three
> are gathered in my name, I'm there with them.'
> Then Peter said to Jesus, 'Lord, how many times
> should I forgive my brother or sister who sins
> against me? Should I forgive as many as seven times?'
> Jesus said, 'Not just seven times, but rather as many as seventy-
> seven times ...'[6]

When I was a university chaplain I once arranged a meeting of
students to discuss forming a justice and peace group. We had hoped
for a lot of people. Only six turned up. To encourage myself, I
whispered to my Methodist colleague, 'Well, it's twice as many as
Jesus said you needed.' Glumly he replied, 'Yes; but it's only half
what he got.'

The size of the basic unit of the church is usually exaggerated.
All over the church, numbers are inflated because we all love to be
part of something big and successful. Most clergy tend to give their
numbers the benefit of the doubt – 'We had at least a hundred, I
would think. Oh, at least. Put down 120'. Meanwhile Jesus promised
he would be there among two or three. Perhaps he was not talking
about a minimum number, but a maximum?

In any case a community of the face must be around a table small
enough for faces to be seen and known.

The apostles were not snooker balls. But if they had been, they
would have been in the right sized group. Twelve is the largest
number of snooker balls which can all touch the same central ball
at the same time.

For people it is not much different. Most group-work studies, in
the church and more widely, would say that eight to fifteen people is
the optimum size for an interactive small group. More than fifteen,
it is good to multiply, to two groups of eight.

As a parish priest I was for ten years in a church which focused
on small group life ('Cell church'). Our cell group leaders were as
worried about numbers as anyone else. But experience cheered
them up. If, on a given week, fewer than usual came ('I'm afraid we

only had five people this week …'), then most often the quality rose ('…but it was such a good meeting!'). And when cell group numbers rose above about fifteen then dissatisfaction rose too ('You can't get a word in edgeways any more … I don't feel I know everyone so well … there's no room now for me to bring my friends … when are we going to multiply?').

When the Bible speaks of the seventy (or seventy-two) it also says that the Lord sent them out in pairs. *(Luke 10:1)*. But obviously when the church grows to a hundred and twenty *(Acts 1:15)*, to over three thousand *(Acts 2:41)*, to five thousand *(Acts 4.4)*, then the dynamic changes.

I'm asking God for a bigger church so that we can make a bigger difference. And in a group of thirty, or fifty, or two hundred, or a thousand, you can do a great many excellent and fruitful things. All the same, unless that group is subdivided into communities of the face, you can't get round a table. You can't do what Jesus did with his friends, and what I'm talking about here.

'…meeting one another…'

In 1916 Martin Buber began to write his little book *I and Thou*[8]. It remains the most beautiful meditation of the twentieth century on community and dialogue.

Buber speaks of the world, including other people, as being open to us in two ways. We can treat others as things, and relate to them as 'I' to 'It'. Or we can treat the others as unique beings, relating to them as 'I' to 'You'.

Many times a day we have to do the first of these. On the day I draft this my windscreen is chipped, and is cracking. I telephone the insurance helpline and, polite though I am, I relate to the assistant there as 'It'. He can help me; it's what he is there for. I am his client, indirectly I pay his wages. I give him my details, we chat briefly about the weather, we say goodbye. There has been a transaction marked by courtesy, but no meeting. There is nothing wrong with this way of relating, and it happens all the time.

But for Buber there is more in life. In every encounter there is the potential for dialogue. 'In all the seriousness of truth, listen.

Without "It" a human being cannot live. But whoever lives only with that is not human.'[9]

Although the 'I-It' encounters keep us alive, it is the 'I-You' encounters that make our life worth living. Buber says, 'I require a You to become; becoming I, I say "You". All real living is meeting.'[10]

These moments of encounter and dialogue are not uncommon. Indeed they fill the world. The week before last in a large, 'faceless' church congregation a woman turns to her neighbour and his noisy child in the pew behind, with a smile. Last week, in one of the churches I've visited while on sabbatical, I turn to my restless neighbour who tells me nervously that she is going into hospital on Thursday for radiotherapy. I squeeze her arm, tell her I'll remember. In moments like that the community of the face is briefly seen.

This is beautiful, this too is normal. There is nothing especially religious about it. Indeed, in the minds of many who are not Christians, the church might almost be defined as a place where you never find it.

There are many churches where the beauty of ordered and reverent worship blends seamlessly with a tolerant and open welcome and a warm humanity. But in other places there seems to be a law of the spirit, that seeking performative excellence diminishes the warmth of meeting. The Denver Lutheran Nadia Bolz-Weber says of her church community, 'We're anti-excellence and pro-participation'. Her church is called The House For All Sinners And Saints. Its self-description: 'a group of folks figuring out how to be a liturgical, Christo-centric, social justice-oriented, queer-inclusive, incarnational, contemplative, irreverent, ancient/future church with a progressive but deeply rooted theological imagination.'[11] It sounds like a church where I might feel at home.

St Paul said 'Let all things be done decently and in order'[12]. It is a Biblical injunction, and refers to a good thing. However, human warmth has been seen by many in the churches to jeopardise this good thing. And so, up and down the country and across the world for hundreds of years, Paul's words have justified a lot of narrow glares and shush-ing on Sunday mornings.

We all know or have heard of moments, of whole churches, where noisy children never receive a smile but only ever a look; where parishioners die of cancer before anyone in the church has noticed that they are ill; where the glory of a brittle beauty has replaced the mess of life. These churches have failed, no matter how beautiful the worship they offer.

But even in church life finds a way, and the sharing of lives is very hard to prevent. You can't catch water with a sieve unless you freeze it first. And even the most forbidding churches are not cold enough to freeze the community of the face altogether.

These glimmerings of warmth between individuals in larger groups are sparks of the Spirit. They are enough to provide the necessary minimum – but only for a moment. Then they go out. Once again, we become atoms in the crowd.

Buber again: 'This is the sadness of our situation … every "You" is doomed to become "It", to become a thing again, even though it may be a noble thing.'[13] Week by week in the communities of Jesus you can see the sparks of the Spirit when people smile across the pews or reach out to another. They are light, and bright, and loving – and they soon go out. Something more is needed if the sparks are to kindle the coals of people's lives and transform them. We need a table to meet around.

The meeting around the table, to which Jesus calls his friends, gives space for this kindling. It builds on the sparkling of this natural sharing, on the way we are, and it goes beyond it. Jesus asks his friends for more than simply being open to others in our day to day lives. He asks for a commitment to belonging.

'…with a durable honesty…'

The community that Jesus gave his friends is marked by a durable honesty – that is, by relationships lived with *permanence* and with a certain *intensity*. To meet like this goes against the grain of our culture.

Today in the West we have chosen a society that is ironic, fluid and radically individualistic. In our sort of society, committing yourself to any formal association is not valued any more. In Robert Putnam's phrase, we are all bowling alone.[14] Clubs, groups, the British Legion, political parties, brass bands, churches – all of them are struggling to survive. This has had an impact on the quality of all our relationships. It has also made the lifestyle of Jesus' group seem very strange.

Meeting with a durable honesty is not linked to any particular way of doing things. But it must be intentional. It has been wisely said of prayer that 'You can't pray everywhere all the time, unless you pray somewhere for some of the time'. Similarly you can't expect to live the lifestyle of Jesus' group unless your diary contains a time and a place for meeting, and your address book contains the people you will meet there.

Obviously, anyone who is committed to this has chosen some way or another. As a parish priest I was committed to small-group life through the structure of cell church. As a bishop the scheduling is harder, but not impossible. The thing itself, although demanding, does not demand any one method.

I stress this for a reason. Graham Pulkingham, like many pioneers of the carpenter's table, opened his home to others in his community, and together with his family he lived in an 'extended family' for some years. This was done in a context of other extended families, all centred around his 'neighbourhood parish'.[15] In the 1960s and 1970s these things did not seem so strange, and God certainly blessed them, for a season.

Forty years later our culture has changed again. People may now be put off the thought of 'intense and permanent' sharing because they might think that the only way to put it all into practice is to live in a commune, or an open-house lifestyle, as Pulkingham did, and as today people attempt to do, in Liverpool and elsewhere.

People keep trying it. In England in the 1970s David Watson did so, with some success at first and much difficulty later. He writes about this in his autobiography.[16] In the Roman Catholic Church Michael Hollings was trying something similar in central London, with the same sort of mixed results.[17] Graham Pulkingham's own story in his later years tells of the pain and risks of living this particular communal lifestyle.

So if you talk about meeting with permanence and intensity today, people begin to shuffle. It all gets lumped in with a gloomy re-assessment of the late 1960s and its many failed experiments in communal living.

But I want to stress that durable honesty in meeting does not depend on any particular method or style. It is the genuine sharing of life in some form that is essential.

For me the words mean something quite simple.

'*Durable*' means that I commit myself to some other Christians, and I do not go away from them even though our relationship may sometimes be difficult.

'*Honesty*' means that I try not to pretend.

All over the church, with an extraordinary variety, people are trying to live like this to this day. Their efforts are not in vain, and the life they live changes them.

'...so that they know life-changing friendship leading to repentance and ministry'

The life flows that way. Friendship – repentance – ministry.

A word first about repentance.

As many sermons have told us, Greek words for repentance, *metanoia, epistrephein*, mean 'changing the mind', 'turning round'.[18] But, try as we may in the church to take this seriously, we always seem to end up by treating repentance as a masochistic, gloomy business. It seems to involve imposing low self-esteem or even self-hatred. It suffers from overtones of Uriah Heep ('I am so very, 'umbly, sorry').

I am not saying that repentance is fun, or that the pain of it can be glossed over. True compunction is liberating, and it can be properly humiliating to see yourself clearly. In the Orthodox churches they speak of 'penthos', the gift of tears, the welling-up of a liberating and healing self-awareness. But the Uriah Heep syndrome must be broken. It is the delight of God to wipe away all tears from our weeping eyes.[19] So when I talk about 'repentance' here, I mean something closer to 'openness' or 'self-disclosure' or 'authenticity'. Its opposite is not 'pride', but 'pretending'.

As the first disciples came to the table, came to know Jesus with permanence and intensity, they were led beyond any pretending.

> He got into one of the boats, the one belonging to Simon, and asked him to put out a little way from the shore....

> ... he said to Simon, 'Put out into the deep water and let down your nets for a catch.' Simon answered, 'Master, we have worked all night long but have caught nothing. Yet if you say so, I will let down the nets.' ... they caught so many fish that their nets were beginning to break ... But when Simon Peter saw it, he fell down at Jesus' knees, saying, 'Go away from me, Lord, for I am a sinful man!' For he and all who were with him were amazed at the catch of fish that they had taken; and so also were James and John, sons of Zebedee, who were partners with Simon. Then Jesus said to Simon, 'Do not be afraid; from now on you will be catching people.'[20]

Religious systems have usually told people to repent first, before they can know God. This seems only fair if you think justice has always to do with retribution, that someone has to take the blame, that forgiveness must always be paid for by the hurting of someone or other. But the result is that a shadow falls. People feel unworthy. They do not want to be close to God because of their sin, which goodness knows is real enough.

Jesus came at this the other way round.
Friendship –

> Jesus boarded one of the boats, the one that belonged to Simon, then asked him...

– repentance –

> Simon Peter...he fell at Jesus' knees and said, 'Leave me, Lord, for I'm a sinner!'

– ministry.

> Then Jesus said to Simon, 'Don't be afraid. From now on, you will be fishing for people.'

It happens wherever Jesus is.
Friendship –

> ... Jesus was tired from his journey, so he sat down at the well. It was about noon. A Samaritan woman came to the well to draw water. Jesus said to her, 'Give me some water to drink.'

His disciples had gone into the city to buy him some food. The Samaritan woman asked, 'Why do you, a Jewish man, ask for something to drink from me, a Samaritan woman?'

– repentance –

... The woman said, 'Sir, I see that you are a prophet ...'

– ministry.

The woman put down her water jar and went into the city. She said to the people, 'Come and see a man who has told me everything I've done! Could this man be the Christ?' They left the city and were on their way to see Jesus.[21]

Wherever Jesus is.
Friendship –

When Jesus came to that spot, he looked up and said, 'Zacchaeus, come down at once. I must stay in your home today.' So Zacchaeus came down at once, happy to welcome Jesus.

– repentance –

Zacchaeus stopped and said to the Lord, 'Look, Lord, I give half of my possessions to the poor...'

– ministry.

...'And if I have cheated anyone, I repay them four times as much.'[22]

In the Gospels men and women drift – just drift – into relationship with the Shepherd, the Beautiful One, drawn by his extraordinary attractiveness, like the Bisto Kids in the gravy advertisement of my childhood, scenting life and following their noses. Once with him in the shallows of relationship they follow Jesus step by step, until they are in the place of no pretending. They find themselves as it were off the edge of the coastal shelf, swimming above fathomless depths. Out-of-my-depth is the experience of repentance. This is the moment when Adam hid himself in the garden because he knew that he was naked.[23]

But in the New Covenant, when the moment of repentance comes, it is too late to hide. By then the disciples already knew Jesus, and even as they turned away to hide, they knew that there was no need; that he saw them as his friends.

Being known by God brings judgement and mercy. In Jesus, God's mercy is offered in the form of friendship. His judgement comes in the form of truthfulness. By his truthfulness we can see ourselves straight, and therefore we can choose to ask God to turn our minds around. It's our choice. The friendship comes first.

> Their worth was not the condition of Jesus' fellowship with his disciples: Judas experienced the same personal involvement that Peter and John did. In the last analysis Judas refused repentance.[24]

Judas refused repentance, and so could no longer see Jesus except in a role. But Jesus did not refuse Judas. His friendship was not withdrawn:

> Just then [Judas] came to Jesus and said, 'Hello, Rabbi.' Then he kissed him. But Jesus said to him, 'Friend, do what you came to do.' Then they came and grabbed Jesus and arrested him.[25]

So the necessary practice for meeting at the table and watching in the moment is *two, three or more Christians meeting one another with a durable honesty, so that they know life-changing friendship leading to repentance and ministry.* But what do I mean by 'necessary'?

Optional?

Christians are depressingly good at deciding what one has to do to be first class. Receive a sacrament from the validly ordained. Speak in tongues. Pray every day. Read your Bible. Join a lively church. Become a member of Amnesty International. Go on retreat. Join a Pride march. Sign a Statement of Faith. Attend a conference or a festival. Get a theology degree. Whatever.

It is odious to divide Christians into first and second classes. But what if Christians themselves come to ask what they need to grow in their faith?

Well, for inward growth in Christ and outwardly to see more people knowing Jesus, more justice in the world, I am recommending the four dimensions in this book: Meet at the table, drink from the fountain, watch for the moment, stretch for the kingdom. Each of them is deeply traditional, though emphasising the table – that is, permanent and intense small-group meeting – seems both foundational and strangely optional.

There has been little controversy in the church's history about what you might call the introverts' disciplines. For example personal private prayer, or disciplined Bible reading, have been seen as pretty central, even essential, if you want to follow Jesus well. This is so even if you are the sort of person who finds reading difficult, or who doesn't like to be on your own. Spiritual practice brings with it spiritual discipline. So Christians are exhorted to chew the dry bread of prayer and Bible study, and we are rightly told that the Holy Spirit will release the goodness as they do. I make that exhortation myself in this book, because I know the value of it.

So the introverts' disciplines are a good thing, and bear fruit in people's lives. And all the disciplines of the spirit are properly offered by the Church to help us grow. Jesus himself plainly assumed prayer, almsgiving and fasting to be part of his hearers' lifestyle:

> 'Whenever you give to the poor ... When you pray ... when you fast ...'[26]

Meanwhile in the Church of England small-group life, like fasting, has always been seen as an optional extra for particularly keen Christians. Or perhaps for people who like that sort of thing – extraverts, people who enjoy meetings. But why have we chosen to put our disciplines in this order?

The writer to Hebrews exhorts Christians:

> And let us consider each other carefully for the purpose of sparking love and good deeds. Don't stop meeting together with other believers, which some people have got into the habit of doing. Instead, encourage each other, especially as you see the day drawing near.[27]

For this writer, meeting together is a discipline. What sort of meeting is in their mind? Well, the writer does not say. Preachers today usually apply the words to Sunday services. But in my own life I know that am provoked to love and good deeds, not as a cog in a large celebration, but as a friend in a small group.

What if you are an introvert? I myself am one, in fact. I find groups difficult. Well, then I have to be disciplined. I turn up anyway. I remember to chew on the dry bread. I trust that the Holy Spirit will release goodness to me. And the discipline bears fruit in my life.

Is any part of the church's life optional? Of course it is. It all is. Practice does not make perfect; God makes perfect. Our Lord has said 'My grace is enough for you'[28]. Christians live in the freedom for which Christ has set us free.

So small-group life is optional? Of course. And still optional if I want to grow as a Christian? Yes, if prayer is. Yes, if regularly receiving Communion is. Yes, if seeking justice is. Yes, if Bible reading is.

Do not strive

> And the servant of the Lord must not strive; but be gentle unto all...[29]

Does all this talk of disciplines, watching, stretching, sound like hard work? I hope not. Jesus said, You did not choose me, but I have chosen you and appointed you to go and bear fruit.[30] The less we sweat it, the more it works. Don't push the river; it flows by itself. We live in a time of spin. Image and presentation are big business. In such a society it is hard to believe that all God asks is that we should be open. And yet, even now, it is almost impossible to over-estimate the attractive power of a life honestly lived. Thomas Merton speaks for us all when he says:

> In an age when there are great demands on us to 'be ourselves', I reserve the right not to worry about being myself, since there is in any case little chance that I can be anybody else.[31]

Jesus is present by his Spirit when two or three gather in his name. He is visibly present at the table if those who gather are transparent. We are not called to be searchlights, but windows. Windows, then, but not ever-open windows. Honesty does not tell us to share what we do not want to share. That would be dishonest.

The Holy Spirit reveals the truth about a person. It is not the job of other Christians to do so. If I am a Christian, at the table with Jesus, the demand of durable honesty is made on me alone. Insofar as I am faithful to that demand – insofar as I stop pretending as I am and stay with people as they are – to that extent the attractiveness of Jesus Christ will be manifest in my life.

Friendship – repentance – ministry. It happens in families, in one-to-one partnerships, in groups.

Imagine for example some Christians in England, in the twenty-first century, trying to meet with a durable honesty. In other words, a bunch of ordinary people getting together in a front room in your street or maybe a one-room flat; meeting most weeks, when they're not on holiday, or ill or something.

John Wesley developed 'class meetings' as a central part of the Methodist movement in the eighteenth century. Small groups of believers met regularly, usually weekly. During each meeting four questions were answered by everyone. They were as follows:

> What known sins have you committed since we last met? What temptations have you faced? How were you delivered from these temptations? What have you thought, said, or done, of which you are uncertain whether it be sin or not?

Perhaps someone in this little group had read that. Or perhaps someone had heard of the East African Revival of the 1940s and 1950s, with its emphasis on 'meeting for fellowship … not insisting on our own rights … and walking in the light – being open about our motives, intentions and actions'.[32] Or maybe they just read the Bible.

Anyway there they are, in the front room. One week someone comes along, invited by a friend. In his life he wants to find out whether God is real. Coming along here is part of that. He is a bit nervous because although he trusts his friend, he is not sure about these other Christians. But he is surprised and relieved. Mostly the meeting is coffee, laughter, talk about cars, clothes, politics, families, sickness, problems, football, decisions; and then the conversation gets around to life. What's up? Any problems?

Friendship –

I like these guys. They're talking about themselves, not about me, and there's none of that miserable sinner stuff I was afraid of. Plus they drink a decent lager. People of discernment.

After a week or two:

Hey. These people are getting really personal in front of me. They don't mind that I'm hearing them. They must trust me. I remember we said things would be confidential, but they obviously believe it. They're supposed to be Christians and now and again they talk about things that I never thought possible of them. They really think God is helping them with some of this stuff, but they don't mind saying if they're stuck. Where are all the hypocrites?

– Repentance –

These questions are a bit sharp. I'll answer them in my head. If you think I'm going to say anything aloud, you can whistle Dixie.

After a week or two:

I can do this in-my-head stuff at home. Time to speak up. Let me censor what I say aloud so that I look honest.

Mm. Sounds good!

After a week or two:

What's the point of coming here every week just to fake it?

After a week or two:

Bloody hell! I need some help with this issue. I'm going to share it.

After a week or two:

I'm going to share it … No. I'll have a go at talking to God about it at home. Safer.

After a week or two:

I'm going to sh … Oh. What? He's struggling with it too. I thought he was really mature! Just goes to show.

Ministry –

Hey – you know what you were saying? I've been into that for years. It's horrible, isn't it? These last couple of weeks I've been – well, sort of praying about it. If you come at it this way it sometimes helps …

Life happens

What happens in such a group? Life happens. The life of the disciples, their meals, their jealousies and squabbles, their parties, their travels, their worries about sick relatives, their work, their shared hopes, the demands made on them. This life was not 'religious life'. It was their common life.

As Bishop David Pytches used to say, 'The meeting place is the training place for the marketplace.'[33] I didn't invent the example above to provide fool proof hints for Christian home groups. I'm just trying to show what it might be like in one place where the carpenter's table has been extended; where the attractiveness and compelling challenge of the person of Jesus Christ is made manifest in his friends.

> There is a tale that a man inspired by God once went out from the creaturely realms into the vast waste. There he wandered until he came to the gates of the mystery. He knocked. From within came the cry: 'What do you want here?' He said, 'I have proclaimed your praise in the ears of mortals, but they were deaf to me. So I come to you that you yourself may hear me and reply.' 'Turn back', came the cry from within. 'Here is no ear for you. I have sunk my hearing in the deafness of mortals.'[34]

The Spirit of God calls things into being that do not exist.[35] Among these is a quality of relationship in the Church where two or three gather together with a durable honesty. In my own life as a believer nothing has drawn me more authentically into God's presence than the table of the poor Christ. By this quality we know the real, supernatural presence of Jesus at that table.

I say 'supernatural', but I do not want to be misunderstood as idealistic. A thing is idealistic if it excludes the cross-grained humanity of human beings from the picture. The work of the Spirit of Jesus is indeed supernatural, but people and their given humanity are always central to it.

The dark night of the group

In a television interview the Russian Orthodox Archbishop Anthony Bloom said 'Many times I meet people who say to me, "I love Orthodoxy, but I can't stand Russians". I say to them, "There is no place for you here. Go!"'

I love Orthodoxy, but I can't stand Russians. I love the carpenter's table; it's just the people sitting there that make it a bit tricky.

You meet weekly in your small group, in a little town in the south of England.

Perhaps the group is inter-generational. This means that there are children there, full members of the small group. These kids do not know how to pretend to be religious. The group meets on a Friday, so that they can stay up a bit later. But it's the end of the week. Now if the children have had a bad week, they will simply make religious activities impossible for everyone else. You try to sing, to pray, to share your heart, all with a shuffling, wriggling, squirming racket going on around you. Idealistic? It doesn't feel like that.

Perhaps the group is adult-only. It is stuck. It has been meeting for a long time. Everyone knows everyone. No one else seems to want to come. The same individuals bring the same stuckness, week after week. You pray for them. The following week, here they are again. And here you are. And missing another good documentary on BBC2. Idealistic? Well, perhaps.

The joy of small-group life can be intense. Its reality, however, is to do with the will, not the emotions.

Splendidly shining darkness[36]

What I am talking about is watching in the moment, like the contemplative prayer I discuss later. Looking to God in silence, with longing love, thinking only of Him. It sounds good. It sounds exalted. It seems worth doing. So you try it. You sit or kneel, shut your eyes, pray silently. You feel pretty holy at first. But soon it gets harder. Then it does not feel exalted at all. You seek God with all your strength but your mind wanders, sometimes you feel grumpy, or bored. Distractions come flooding in. Surely you must be doing it wrong? No. The Christian mystics talk about the dark night of the senses, and the dark night of the soul. But surely they can't mean my grumpy boredom?

Can they not? Ruth Burrows says, of moments like that:

> What is the essence of your grief, when all is said and done? Isn't it two things; a sense that you lack God … and at the same time a devastating awareness of your own wretchedness? Oh, I know, not in the least like what St John of the Cross writes about, that is what you are hastening to tell me, nothing grandiose like that, just drab petty meanness and utter ungodliness. Yes, but that *is* what he is talking about.[37]

Life happens. Rowan Williams comments:

> It is important to note that John [of the Cross] is not discussing a merely 'spiritual' or internal condition, [but is talking about]…the reduction of spirituality to nothing… nothing else can serve as a preparation for the authentic union of the self with God.[38]

Like prayer itself, the life of Jesus' group promises no lovely feelings, though it provides them from time to time. It *promises* only that God will be present.

By my Spirit

> 'If one of you wanted to build a tower, wouldn't you first sit down and calculate the cost, to determine whether you have enough money to complete it? Otherwise, when you have laid the foundation but couldn't finish the tower, all who see it will begin to belittle you. They will say, "Here's the person who began construction and couldn't complete it!"'[39]

In my Christian life I have often been impulsive, romantic, quixotic, too hasty to respond to whatever I think God might be asking of me. Most of us believers could say the same. We want 'to give God everything' and we rarely heed the words of Jesus that we must count the cost first.

Sometimes, though, you come to prayers that force you to take stock. You have to admit to God that you are afraid to pray them. For me this has happened three times in thirty years.

The first is John Wesley's covenant prayer:

> I am no longer my own, but yours. Put me to what you will, rank me with whom you will. Put me to doing, put me to suffering. Let me be taken up for you or laid aside for you...[40]

The second is the prayer of abandonment by Charles de Foucauld:

> I surrender myself into your hands. Do with me what you will. Whatever you do, I will thank you. Let only your will be done in me, as in all your creatures, and I'll ask nothing more, my Lord...[41]

And the third is this from Graham Pulkingham, where as he prays he hears God say:

> 'You must love with my love, suffer with my suffering, forgive with my forgiveness in the places where I send you...you've asked me to open their blind eyes and deaf ears and to soften their hardened hearts. I'll do it, all of it – at your hands. I'm offering you grace enough for that. But grace of this kind is costly, not like the grace I give for yourself. It's free for them, but if you continue to serve me in the needs of these people, in one way or another I'll require your life at their hands.'
>
>   'How can these things be?' My heart pleaded with earnestness.
>
>   'By my Spirit.'[42]

At the table of the poor carpenter, these prayers are prayed. The One who calls us there and sits beside us there, is the One also who sends us from there and accompanies us, so that we can return with new friends to join the community of his friends, and so that by listening to and working with those who live on the edge of things, we can see the world he loves transformed.

6. Drinking from the fountain

The holy table

Jesus answered, 'Everyone who drinks this water will be thirsty again, but whoever drinks from the water that I will give will never be thirsty again. The water that I give will become in those who drink it a spring of water that bubbles up into eternal life.'[1]

On the last and most important day of the festival, Jesus stood up and shouted, 'All who are thirsty should come to me! All who believe in me should drink! As the scriptures said concerning me, Rivers of living water will flow out from within…' Jesus said this concerning the Spirit…[2]

The highest excellence is like that of water. The excellence of water appears in its benefiting all things, and in its occupying, without striving to the contrary, the low place which all people dislike. Hence its way is near to that of the Way (Tao).[3]

The biblical Gospel

If you sit with him at the table, then the One who made it will feed and nourish you, day by day and week by week. You will be fed by the poor carpenter with his own body and blood, and nourished through the company you keep there, and given to drink from the fountain of life. That is a fountain of thought and story and image and song, and we find it in the Bible, and in the creeds and liturgies of the church, and in the reflections and prayers of those who went before us and who come around us. This is the language that the Church speaks. Bible and creeds and liturgies are not summaries of longer and more systematic teaching. They are themselves the vessels of revelation and of the setting forth of revelation, and Christians are called to speak their language and to return to it daily.

Our Rule of Life in Liverpool diocese says that we are called to pray, read, and learn. I hope that all those who sit at the table will hear that call, returning again and again to the Bible and the creeds and the prayers of the church, praying and reading and learning together.

As an Anglican/Episcopalian I look to the Bible as uniquely revealing the saving truth about God, to the agreed creeds of the early Church as setting forth that truth, to the agreed liturgy of the Church as embodying and enacting the truth, and to certain historic Anglican documents as bearing witness to all this in theology and tradition. The image this brings to mind is of a powerful wellspring (of inspired revelation), which is then shaped and channelled by the prayers and reflections of those who have come before us on this journey, so that the living water cascades as from a fountain. And as we sit at the table together we can be nourished by fresh and clear and life-giving water, the water that has been collected from this fountain.

Everyone grows up within a tradition of thought and opinion, or chooses such a tradition in adult life. Specific ways of believing – avenues of reflection on scripture, creeds, history – enrich the Church and feed us all as we reflect on them and share them together. These traditions of opinion have an honoured place. They are crucial for our developing understanding. But they are all partial and none of them can replace the rich and textured 'mere Christianity' of the sources themselves, both written and enacted.

This is why I dislike the use of the phrase 'wrestling with scripture' as a description of what happens when we read the hard bits in the Bible. Jacob wrestled with an angel, not a book. There are better metaphors for our relationship with the Bible than one drawn from competitive sport. I do not remember 'wrestling' with English when as a tiny child I learned it, hard though it may be to speak well, and hard though languages are to learn for most adults. Jesus said that we should become as a little child,[4] and perhaps his words apply here. The wellsprings of our faith constitute a language and we are called to speak it, and the aim of our discipleship is to speak as natives speak, by total immersion. This is true even though the language of scripture and creed can appear counter-culturally odd or unclear or unsophisticated, even naïve. In his wonderful 1930s book *The Gospel and the Catholic Church*, speaking of the rich and poetic phrases of the Creeds, Michael Ramsey has this to say:

> The biblical Gospel has overcome the speculative mind. And the simple, pictorial language of 'he came down,' 'he ascended,' is not the language of a time or of a school of thought, but the inescapable language of the human race and of common

life. Language less 'mythological' in form is less permanent. A Creed that substituted for these pictorial phrases the language of 'modern thought' or of any scheme of thought would be the Creed of an ephemeral scholasticism, and not the Creed of a Gospel before which all scholasticisms must bow.[5]

If this is so, then the spiritual discipline (the religious practice) that matters most is to be totally immersed, over and over again, in the real thing – the scriptures, the creeds, the liturgies of the Church. This is what I mean by drinking from the fountain. Bottled theological water, with artificial bubbles or an arbitrary choice of vitamins, is no substitute for the sources. Speaking of the growth of the church, George Lindbeck caught the truth of this:

> Pagan converts to the Catholic mainstream did not, for the most part, first understand the faith and then decide to become Christians; rather, the process was reversed: they first decided and then they understood. More precisely, they were first attracted by the Christian community and form of life. Only after they had acquired proficiency in the alien Christian language and form of life were they deemed able intelligently and responsibly to profess the faith, to be baptised.[6]

In short, I am grateful for the community of learning from which I received the tools for biblical study and analysis, and I am glad to use them as part of who I am. But first and foremost there is a language to learn, and to speak. And so I am also grateful for Ramsey's words, and for these from Leander Keck:

> It is now time! Time to stop worrying about the Bible and to start worrying about ourselves. Time to stop using the Bible and to start living with it. And time to stop telling the Bible what it means and to let its mythological character restore imagination to our thought and praise.[7]

Flowing water

The substance H_2O is essential to life. It is almost unique, in that human beings can easily access it in each of its three forms. Solid, liquid and gas; water, ice and steam. That this is so is a gift of God. But of the three forms it is only water that sustains life. If you're stranded on an ice floe, or indeed in a Turkish bath, you will not live for many days unless you can melt the ice or condense the steam into water once again. Similarly, Christian teaching can come to me as ice, hard and unyielding and sharp; or as steam, vague and obscuring and misty; or as water, nourishing and clear. If I'm to get nourishment from the elements of the faith, I must receive them in the form that flows – as liquid.

And if I am to drink deeply from the fountain I have to trust that the source is wholesome; that is to say, that the Bible nourishes life. I am convinced that it does. If I were not, I would not have chosen to read it every day for almost fifty years. Scripture is fathomless, sublimely beautiful, pellucid in its understanding of human life, golden in its illumination of the Lord Jesus and of the God who he is and whom he reveals. It is complex, almost unimaginably rich, capable of revealing new truth on each reading, as the highlighter of the Holy Spirit emphasises now this, now that passage or word. And it comes to me as water and not as ice, or steam. That is to say, it comes to me as nourishment and not like a stone, or like a mist. Like water (as Lao Tzu said) it can flow and fill and take the lowest place, meeting me where I am in my brokenness and in my need.

The Bible speaks very little about itself. When it does, it is at once confident and modest about its own purpose.

> Every scripture is inspired by God and is useful for teaching, for showing mistakes, for correcting, and for training character, so that the person who belongs to God can be equipped to do everything that is good.[8]

I believe that Holy Scripture contains all things necessary for salvation, as the Thirty-Nine Articles say. The Articles also describe the Bible, crisply and unforgettably, as 'God's word written'. This sounds comfortingly straightforward, but the fact is that God has not written God's word as an absolute and unambiguous list of things to think and do. There are many who indeed wish we had such a Bible, unambiguous in every verse. And there are of course some who believe that we do indeed possess such a book; though people who agree on that can find it harder to agree on precisely what the book means, in this or that place.

The Bible touches the heart as liquid and not solid; the ice of writing softened by the breath of the Spirit. As the evangelical scholar Roger Beckwith has said: '*God's revelation is wholly inapprehensible apart from the saving work of the Holy Spirit in [a person's] heart. It is through the Spirit's work that [an individual] is personally confronted with God as Creator and Redeemer.*'[9]

It has always been a temptation for Christians to carve and shape scripture like an ice sculpture, to freeze and smooth and simplify and harmonise its sometimes-turbulent message. For myself I am relaxed about the ambiguities and difficulties of scripture, because I believe that all of it is breathed by God, and that God knows what God is doing, and therefore that an ambiguous and sometimes difficult book is what God wanted us to have. And to drink at the fountain is, more than anything, to read this book, open to the Spirit's work in the mind and heart, to read it and reread it, over and over again.

One of the great strengths of the Anglican/Episcopalian tradition is that it asks its people to read a lot of scripture, and to move beyond favourite passages or themes into parts of the Bible we would not normally visit by ourselves. Tricky and unfamiliar bits of the Bible can raise tricky and unfamiliar questions. And if our reading produces questions, this is good, because questions are what curiosity sounds like.

Of course it is not always the case that each question can be quickly and satisfactorily answered. In fact the best questions often can't be. In my own life it's the unanswered questions that have helped me to grow most. Which way is up? What on earth am I doing on earth? Why is life so painful so often? Why can't I ask my Mum and Dad these questions, since they are dead? Why do so many children not have a Mum and Dad to ask from the beginning?

I have heard lots of answers to questions like this, some very glib and clear. But any answers that seek to remove the mystery from the questions have come to me as ice (too hard to help) or mist (too vague to help) rather than as thirst-quenching water. C. S. Lewis wrote two books on the reality of evil and grief in the world: *The Problem of Pain* (1940) which is a detached and scholarly review of evil as a problem, and *A Grief Observed* (1961) which is a record of his anguished struggle after the death of his wife, a struggling with evil as a mystery. Many people have indeed been helped by

The Problem of Pain, though in my language it is a glittering ice sculpture. But it is *A Grief Observed*, which Lewis published under a pseudonym so that it would come to people afresh, that spoke and still speaks about the reality of death, bringing water to those in the desert of their own bereavement, as it did to me after my mother died.

I need water and not ice; I need God's revelation neat and not on the rocks. Too often I have sat in churches and had the Bible mansplained to me, as if God's word were a stagnant pool that can't flow by itself, needing a theological stir, or a doctrinal push. And yet when the living water is permitted to flow, and when preachers have evidently immersed themselves in it, and are splashing and rippling the living water so that I can see anew the way it catches the light and fills the cup, then even without an answer my deepest thirst has been quenched and I have been strengthened to keep on living with the questions that my complicated life, and the complicated Bible itself, has given me.

Here is another analogy. In her fine book *Virtuoso Theology* Professor Frances Young presents a wonderful perspective on scriptural study and exposition, exploring the interpretation of a text as if it were great music, as if theologians were performance artists. My own first degree was in a performance art – drama – and so I resonate deeply with her analogy. It is possible to interpret a text conservatively or radically, helpfully or unhelpfully. Two performances of the same score, or text, can be so different as to seem to be based on different works. Fashions in performance, just as in Biblical interpretation, come and go. Questions of faithfulness to the score or text are embraced by all performance artists, and answered differently by them all. And yet, as the theatre director Peter Brook used to say, at the end of the evening the text is still there, and no one has destroyed it. So it is with reading the Bible. The simplicity of some texts poses a question of application to the reader; have you done this simple thing in your own life; loved your enemy, dealt with your anger before the sun goes down, prayed in the words Jesus taught you? The difficult gnarliness of other texts is an invitation to the reader to ask yet more questions of fact or of interpretation; what is the abomination of desolation, how should I turn the other cheek, why did Jesus die?

You may have made it a rule to pray and read and learn. You may have read or heard the word of God in scripture, and have attempted to form your life by that word. You may have been moved from time to time to ask what on earth that word means. And if you have brought these things to the carpenter's table and shared them there with the friends of God, then the life of the accountable Church has been fulfilled once again in your life.

For most of us in the West, it is not hard to read or hear the Bible. The task of making the word of God accessible to all is very well advanced. Drinking from the fountain daily is a daily possibility, for all who can read, or hear. And sharing what you have read or heard, and so deepening it, is daily possible too. Speaking out of the lyrical Methodist tradition, the tradition that was born in song, Frances Young says this better than I can:

> We are invited not just to hear but to respond, to listen to the voice of our Beloved, and filled with exultation sing our love-songs. For that is spirituality - thinking, feeling, and acting in love and singing praises to our Divine Lover. When we sing love-songs we may use the classical scores of scripture or tradition, or we may make our own improvisations. But the themes are universal.[10]

We can connect with the creeds, too, reading them and rereading and thinking and asking and growing. We can do so in private, or in public as we read together aloud. I write these words in the United States, where I have been sharing the prayers of the Episcopal Church in a number of cities. The details of the Bible readings differ from my own, though the steady diet of scripture is the same as I am used to in the Church of England. But I have been invited, in the daily prayers of the Episcopal Church, to say the creeds far more frequently than I say them at home. Their *Book of Common Prayer*, like the Church of England's Book of 1662, asks that the creeds be said each morning and evening as a matter of course. And I have done that for a few months. It has done me the world of good.

Drinking from the fountain, then, is sharing in actions wider than the mind and its speculations. Having said that, in writing all this I worry that the sort of thing I'm saying, and the sort of thing

Michael Ramsey said a couple of pages ago, will be misunderstood. I worry that you might think I am saying that scripture and creeds are 'poetic' documents which need not be taken seriously as statements of truth. This is not so, though the truth in scriptures and creeds comes to us gently and subtly, as we make it our own through prayer and practice.

When I was training for ministry in the 1970s, the Doctrine Commission of the Church of England produced 'Christian Believing', a brief report followed by a series of personal essays. Some of my theological heroes were members of this Commission, including Professor John Macquarrie, the great evangelist Michael Green, Canon Donald Allchin and others. Their report was controversial. A good many people received it very poorly, usually on the grounds that it was wishy-washy and overly sceptical. The General Synod was never given the opportunity to debate it. It slipped quite quickly into obscurity. Nonetheless it was in the world, new-minted, when I was at college; and hungry students like me were able to buy it and read it. And I was grateful for it. To this day I find it hard to object to a book that begins: 'Christian life is an adventure, a voyage of discovery, a journey, sustained by faith and hope, towards a final and complete communion with the Love at the heart of all things.'[11]

In its chapter 'The nature of religious language', the Commission faced the question that has worried me:

> It is often loosely remarked nowadays that religious language is 'poetic'. This is a word which can be used so vaguely … that it serves no useful purpose and may even be seriously misleading…
> To say that all religious language is inadequate, or that we are dealing with images and symbols of a transcendent and ultimately inexpressible reality, does not mean that 'anything goes'. It is true that our models … are only pointers; but they do point in certain directions and not in others.'[12]

We can refuse to treat credal statements as icy, but that does not mean we are compelled to see them as misty. However there is no doubt that the creeds have been known to present problems for lots of would-be Christians. 'I want to join the church, but I can't accept …' – the Virgin birth, the Resurrection of the Body, whatever it may be. Some people have chosen, or indeed have been encouraged, metaphorically to cross their fingers while saying parts of the creed, mentally exempting themselves from the words of their community. Those who do this may sometimes feel like people of integrity surrounded by hypocrites, and at other times may feel that they are not trying hard enough to believe and are falling short of the gold standard of faith. Neither feeling is particularly helpful, and both responses emerge from an individualism which the writers of the creeds themselves would not recognise. And indeed the only criticism of 'Christian Believing' that had force for me was that it did not pay enough attention to the fact that as believers we believe in common.

This criticism was swiftly addressed, since the next Doctrine Commission report, from a substantially revised Commission, was called 'Believing in the Church'[13]. This group too contained heroes of mine, including W. H. Vanstone, N. T. Wright, David Jenkins and Bishop John Taylor of Winchester. And its report began with a word from the underground stream – from a lay woman, Dorothy Sayers, and from her poetic play *The Just Vengeance*. An airman dies, and arrives in a heavenly city, and is asked to state his claim to citizenship:

Recorder:
What matters here is not so much what you did
As why you did it … Can you recite your creed?

Airman: I believe in God –

Chorus (picking him up and carrying him along with it):
The Father Almighty, Maker of heaven and earth. And in
Jesus Christ –

Airman:

No! No! No! What made me start off like that?
I reacted automatically to the word 'creed' –
My personal creed is something totally different.

Recorder:

What is speaking in you in the voice of the city,
The Church and household of Christ, your people and
country

From whom you derive. Did you think you were
unbegotten?
Unfranchised? With no community and no past?
Out of the darkness of your unconscious memory
The stones of the city are crying out. Go on.[14]

When I/we say the creed the stones of the city are crying out,
carrying me/us along with it. These are ancient stones, unlike the
'statements of faith' which proliferate and contend with one another
in the marketplace of concepts. I do not say them enough, unlike
my companions in the Episcopal Church. It will be good to be
nourished from the fountain and to say them more, to be pointed in
their direction, without reaching too irritably after fact and reason
as I consider the detail of their meaning, both for those who wrote
them and for me.

I feel the same about the liturgy within which my faith is
expressed. There are many good reasons for having a prayer book,
but the one that matters most to me is that it provides a clear
channel, so that the revelation of the scripture as set forth in the
creeds may be directed daily into my mind and heart. I say the
prayers in the book I have been given. And if I am tempted to
select my favourite prayers from the book, or indeed to select my
favourite prayer book from all the books, I remind myself that it is
the stones of the city – my city – that cry out in my voice through
these prayers in this book; and I stay with it a little longer.

And indeed something of the same is true for the hymns of the
Church. In my tradition it is our prayer book that expresses our
faith, but as with the Methodist people, Anglicanism was born in
song. I write these words on the feast of George Herbert, but I have
a more modern example in mind; the great hymn 'In Christ Alone'
(by Stuart Townend and Keith Getty) which sings of the saving
death of Jesus Christ and declares that on that cross 'The wrath of
God was satisfied'.

Some people refuse to sing these words, changing them
unilaterally even though the writers have asked them not to do so.
Others refuse to sing the hymn at all, on the grounds that it conveys
an offensive understanding of what Jesus did for us on the Cross.
I on the other hand sing the line gladly, though my understanding

of the Atonement is not restricted to the idea that God was forced by God's own sense of justice to punish someone, and out of love chose to punish Jesus for my sake. I think that God is sovereign, and thus more free than that of the demands for punishment. But I know that many of the stones of the city were built by holy people who believed exactly what Townend and Getty write, and that today, among those at the table of the poor carpenter, are millions who believe exactly this too. So I am happy to be borne along by their witness as I sing. In this I agree with the Revd Ian Paul, whose fine blog 'Psephizo' contains an excellent discussion of just this controversy. He says:

> ... truth is not best expressed by a set of propositions alone. God did not make a mistake when he gave us the Scriptures, in all their variety and (apparent) contradictions. And our unity is not found in agreement on a particular statement of doctrine. It is found in the person of Jesus, crucified and risen, whom we proclaim as Lord. Our unity is, in fact, 'in Christ alone'.[16]

The wellspring of scripture, shaped and channelled in creeds and historical formularies, in prayers prayed and songs sung - this is the fountain from which those who sit at the table are given to drink. The gift is wonderful, nourishing and true, and to drink from it daily will set in each one at the table a foundation – a foundation from which they can enter what the early theologians of the church described as prayer.

7. Watching in the moment

The immediate table

At the centre of our being is a point of nothingness which is untouched by sin and by illusion, a point of pure truth, a point or spark which belongs entirely to God, which is never at our disposal, from which God disposes of our lives, which is inaccessible to the fantasies of our own mind or the brutalities of our own will. This little point of nothingness and of absolute poverty is the pure glory of God in us. It is so to speak His name written in us, as our poverty, as our indigence, as our dependence, as our [being His children]. It is like a pure diamond, blazing with the invisible light of heaven. It is in everybody, and if we could see it we would see these billions of points of light coming together in the face and blaze of a sun that would make all the darkness and cruelty of life vanish completely ... I have no program for this seeing. It is only given. But the gate of heaven is everywhere.[1]

For the theologians of the early church, 'prayer' meant two things. Firstly it meant words said and things done, 'saying your prayers', 'doing the liturgy'. The common prayers of the Church will feed us all our lives as we sit at the table. St Benedict understood this when he described the reciting of psalms as a discipline, and had his monks assemble in the chapel together to recite them for hours each day. But alongside and beneath all that, 'prayer' for the early theologians meant a disposition of the mind, something which invested the words said and the things done with divine meaning and transformative power.[2] Those of us who sit with the carpenter at his table will learn this sort of prayer too, the sort of prayer that enables you to watch in the moment.

Prayer like this is not a touchy-feely thing. In the evangelical church of my youth we were taught to imagine three cats on a wall, or in another image we were taught to think of a railway engine, a coal tender and a carriage (it was a long time ago). One of the cats (or the railway engine) was called Faith. Another cat (or the coal tender) was called Facts. The third cat (or the carriage) was called Feelings. The purpose of these images was to teach us that 'feelings follow faith', in other words that the transient emotions and commitments of our life could not take the place of the engine, or could not lead the cats along the wall. Faith as an act of the will, nourished by the facts of our Christian religion as we had received them - these things had the primacy, and feelings needed to know their place and to tag along. There is a good deal of truth in this teaching.

As I apply it to the thinking of the early theologians, it reinforces and underlines the place of faithful habitual action in prayer. I was ordained in June 1979. Between the day of my ordination and the day I write this, 14,140 days have elapsed. On each of these days I have sought to say my prayers, and to read the Bible, as I promised to do. Before that date too I tried to do these things. Sometimes of course I have not done so, for reasons ranging from illness to forgetfulness to laziness. But in the main, like millions of other lay and ordained Christians, I have been able to sustain a pattern of action, reading from a book (or more recently a phone or tablet) and reciting other well-known texts from memory. Whether you call this reciting the Daily Office or having a Quiet Time is not important. You are drinking from the fountain and this leads to formation of the spirit. It is commendable and even essential to anyone who wants to grow in Christ.

Nonetheless this 'vocal prayer' and 'lectio divina' has been seen by the teachers of the church as insufficient unless (as they put it) 'the mind and the heart' also are praying. In the twentieth chapter of his Rule St Benedict says:

> 'Whenever we want to ask some favour of a powerful person, we do it humbly and respectfully, for fear of presumption. How much more important, then, to lay our petitions before the Lord God of all things with the utmost humility and sincere devotion. We must know that God regards our purity of heart and tears of compunction, not our many words. Prayer should therefore be short and pure, unless perhaps it is prolonged under the inspiration of divine grace. In community, however, prayer should always be brief; and when the superior gives the signal, all should rise together.'

Commenting on this the Abbot of the Monastery of Christ in the Desert has this to say: 'The admonition on short prayer in community comes from the way in which our ancestors looked at prayer. Quite often the saying of prayers was seen as distinct from the prayer itself. After saying a prayer, then one prayed in the heart and *this* was considered 'prayer.'[3]

In other words there is indeed something internal to be laid alongside the external faithfulness to a rule of prayer – not at all replacing them, but nonetheless to be distinguished and sought for its own sake. From the underground stream St Teresa of Avila makes the same distinction in her own very direct way:

> You must know, daughters, that whether or not you are practicing mental prayer has nothing to do with keeping the lips closed. If, while I am speaking with God, I have a clear realization and full consciousness that I am doing so, and if this is more real to me than the words I am uttering, then I am combining mental and vocal prayer. When people tell you that you are speaking with God by reciting the Paternoster and thinking of worldly things – well, words fail me.[4]

The idea, then, using my own image, is that we sit at the carpenter's table with our book, phone or tablet and we read of him, or even to him, as he sits beside us so closely. And alongside this, or separate from it, we look to the carpenter, and to his Father, in heart and mind. As the Catholic charismatic Ralph Martin sums it up, 'Prayer is, at root, simply paying attention to God.'[5]

In my own reflection on these things I have come to believe that sitting very close to Jesus at his table, and reading and praying and thinking in the ways described here, can then be placed alongside a way of praying, or being, which I'm calling 'real-time'. Reading and reflecting, praying and thinking, and then watching in real time.

These ways of being there for God are not to be arranged like a flight of steps, whereby you climb (in Latin, 'graduate') from one to the other as if you were getting better at it and so rising in the world of the spirit. No degrees will be awarded in the life of prayer. At the heart of our faith is indeed a beautiful mystery, but it's not the sort of mystery that is reserved for 'experts in the spiritual life', if that phrase means anything at all. (I don't think it does. All I have noticed is that some people have got used to being an utter beginner, having been one for longer.)

Nor does sharing in these practices, and in the real-time moments, depend on membership of any particular Christian tradition. Still less does it depend on any spiritual 'skills' or 'techniques' or 'methods' of prayer – though of course many of these are helpful for those who embrace the living reality of them, in living contact with someone who knows their purpose and their value. And speaking generally as a bishop in a very diverse church I would encourage any reader who wants to find out more about this stuff to talk to the people who sit around the carpenter's table where you are, that is to the people in your local church, in your neighbourhood or network, wherever the Christians gather in your context.

Let me say more though about the real-time moment, because when I speak in this book of 'watching in the moment', it is this moment that I mean.

The moment has a particular flavour and a particular outcome. The flavour is the flavour of companionable emptiness, that is of utter dependence on the God who is not me. We come then to realise that for this moment, and in this moment, the initiative has passed from us to the One we cannot see. We stand in emptiness in the moment. And the outcome is that, for the duration of the moment, we are living in *real time* – experiencing each passing moment for what it is, not leaping ahead or falling behind in the tangle of our thoughts and feelings, in what the teachers of the early Church called our 'passions'. We are there, depending on God, watching for God, waiting on God, waiting for the moment when, as the Psalmist says in a phrase used by the deacon in the Orthodox Communion liturgy, 'it is time for the Lord to act'.

This moment of empty and real-time watching is not mystically exalted and not emotionally exalted either. It can indeed confer great serenity and calm in the heart, but usually that is something that's recognised later, and usually by other people. In the moment itself it does not feel like that. Sitting beside the poor carpenter, gazing with him at whatever is before us, usually feels uncomfortable; hard and awkward and grainy. So at any rate it is for me. Distractions and ideas and thoughts pour in from the future or the past, each one seeking to pull me out of real time.

A good many of these distractions and ideas are impeccably worthy, impeccably Christian, perhaps exalted and theological, perhaps full of wisdom as to how the church can be improved. It can seem inappropriate and rather trivial to set them aside and just to look with Jesus at what is actually there, in real time. But the most exalted distractions have no more value, in this moment with God, than the more mundane ones: the invasion into the mind of the shopping list, the nagging feeling that the oven may still be on, the worry about a child I know, the plight of the refugees I don't know, my irritation with the bloody fool at work who will not do what is so obvious. These too have their place in the world, since remembering the milk, and switching off the oven and caring for the child and loving the displaced and learning to get on with irascible colleagues will all make the world a better place. But connecting with God, the interesting thing about religion, happens in the moment when all these superficially-much-more-interesting things have faded away because they are not in real time, not in this moment, not present now, where God is.

In my own stumbling and wandering way I've tasted its flavour of this moment many times in many ways, and I've seen its outcome right across the traditions of God's people, as they sit beside His Son in the circumstances of their lives.

I have sat alone beside the poor carpenter in the silence of contemplation, when the sound of the bell dies away and the ripples on the stillness fade and for twenty minutes there is no focus but a word in the mind, it may be 'Jesus' or 'Love' or the Aramaic word from the Bible, 'Maranatha': 'Come, Lord', 'The Lord comes'.[6]

I have prayed in the charismatic tradition, speaking to God in a language I do not know, the love-language of tongues, the babbling brook of praise, the welling spring with which the Orthodox in the Philokalia, and the Franciscans in the Little Flowers, and the Pentecostals are alike familiar in their way. I have asked God for the healing of a sick child or a sick friend, and having asked God I have waited in silence and watched my child or my friend, gazing on them as the Christ beside me gazes on them, looking hard for the signs of new strength and of love fulfilled, longing and hoping that they will come.[7]

And in countless services of worship I have sat in silence after the Word of God has been pronounced in preaching and the challenge and consolation of love have been shared, or again after the life of God has been shared in the sacraments, gazing on my own future in the companionable emptiness, in the presence of the invisible Christ, my Lord and my God, the interesting thing about religion.

These moments in worship have prepared me for the other moments, moments of pastoral contact or of social action or of simple human living and dying, all of them moments when the same real-time dynamic applies.

So as a younger priest I have stood shivering in the small hours of the morning outside military bases, in vigil with hundreds of others, Anglicans and Methodists and Quakers and Catholics and agnostics and atheists alike. I have watched the headlights approach over the plain, watched them resolve into the huge vehicles, the convoy of nuclear Cruise missiles passing in the darkness, each one able to destroy life superabundantly. And as I watched in helplessness and in a helpless solidarity, I have prayed that peace might prevail in that moment, in every moment.

So as a University Chaplain I have sat, week by week, with a student struggling with obsessive-compulsive disorder, a young man whose hands were raw because he felt the need to wash and scrub them over and over again, and who asked for help. Week by week we met, for 45 minutes each time, and in all the meetings he never said a word. And at first, remembering all my pastoral training, I tried to make conversation; but soon I too was silent. And the image in my mind was of entering a dark pool, of stillness and helplessness, as he and I sat together in real time, a time of silent attention and intercession. At the end of each session he asked that we should meet again. Each time we lived in the moment of his illness, in a silent solidarity where God was present.

So as a son I have sat beside my father's deathbed, keeping vigil through the night as he gasped for air and struggled to remain alive until the dawn. And my sister shaved him, and we gave him his after-shave so that he smelled good, and holding his hand I prayed for him and then I blessed him with Aaron's blessing: 'The Lord bless you and keep you; the Lord make His face to shine upon you and be gracious to you; the Lord lift up the light of His countenance upon you and give you peace…' and in the moment I prayed the blessing, he died. And I felt an infinite helplessness in the face of death, the most certain of all the things we know. But also a clear sense of living in real time, in the present moment, living each moment of his life, of my life, in the presence of the God of life, in the hope and the victory of the resurrection.

In all these and other ways I have trusted in the presence of the poor carpenter, the invisible and loving God who is as God is in Jesus. And in all these and other ways I have entered again the place of companionable and trusting emptiness, the place of dependence on the One in whom I live and move and have my being. That One was there before words and before certainty, before concept and beyond definition. And I know that hundreds of millions have been in their moment before this moment, and are there in their own moment now and across the world, and will be there with God in their own moment after I too have gone.

Thomas Merton, with whose words I began this chapter, speaks elsewhere of the soul as an infinitely timid wild animal, perhaps like a small deer or a mouse, who will only emerge into the open in the safest and quietest and most tranquil moment. One of the reasons for the Church is to make room for this moment, and to encourage its people to enter it. We are called inward to this place, 'This little point of nothingness and of absolute poverty [which] is the pure glory of God in us'. Only from this place can we venture forth to speak of Jesus and to fight for justice, as the poor carpenter asks us to do. Only from this place, then, can we stretch for the kingdom.

8. Stretching for the Kingdom

More people knowing Jesus

Thomas responded to Jesus, 'My Lord and my God!'[1]

The moment of evangelism is the specific proclamation of the good news of Jesus Christ to another person or people. It is undertaken for God and with God, with news from God about God. There is no greater honour than bearing this Good News to another, no greater privilege than seeing others respond to the Good News, and no greater challenge than to be captivated by the urgency of this vocation.[2]

Singleness of purpose

As we sit and meet at the table of the poor carpenter, we can drink from the fountain and watch in the moment. Alongside this, in the same breath as this, he will invite us to rise and to stretch for the kingdom. His invitation is not one by which we qualify for our seat at the table; he has already given that to us by grace. But it seems to me, and it has certainly been true for me, that the gracious invitation to stretch makes life even more fully worth living. Because it is very good to see more people knowing Jesus and more justice in the world.

As I see it there is a seamless coherence to my four emphases – the seamless unity of companionship at the table, depth in Christian belonging and prayer, and a ceaseless care for wider inclusion in the church. And within the last of my emphases – stretching for the kingdom – I see a real coherence between the call of Christ to share my faith, and the call of the same Christ to struggle for justice, to defend the voiceless and to learn from those on the edge of things, and in particular those neglected or even despised by the churches. I yield to the urging, the constraining power, of the love of Christ for all, of which Paul spoke: 'For the love of Christ urges us on, because we are convinced that one has died for all; therefore all have died. And he died for all, so that those who live might live no longer for themselves, but for him who died and was raised for them.'[3] I am bewildered by those who say that evangelism and an inclusive social justice can operate independently, as if they were multiple-choice questions, elective arms of the churches' witness, rather than aspects of the one mandate. For me then, asking God for a bigger church that makes a bigger difference is one single thing.

Stretching on the labyrinth

'Stretch for the kingdom.' It was in Berkeley, California, that this image of stretching came to me. I remember the occasion rather ruefully. I had contacted the Director of Innovative Ministry at Grace Cathedral, San Francisco, with a request to meet and to find out more about what the Cathedral was doing to connect with its people in evangelism and in social action. He invited me to a number of things, including the very popular 'Yoga on the Labyrinth' which takes place most Tuesday evenings.

Around 800 people, almost all young adults, converge on the Cathedral each week, filling every available space. They are led through a sequence of yoga positions followed by a deep and peaceful time of contemplation. Participants are offered hospitality and a calm spirituality. The place of the Cathedral as a centre for Christian worship is not ignored or minimised. A courteous and fruitful outreach is achieved. Those who later need spiritual and pastoral advice are able to turn to the ministers of the Cathedral they now know. All this sounded good to me, and so, wanting to sustain the good name of the Church of England, I volunteered not only to attend but also to join in. I had not taken part in a yoga session since I was a student, some forty years before.

As far as I could see, I was by at least twenty-five years the oldest person there. Nothing daunted, I stretched and held position with the best of them. My pride in my yoga was somewhat dented, however, when I cracked a rib in attempting one of the poses. The dull sound of the rib cracking was clearly audible around me, and brought me some much-needed compassion from one of my fellow-stretchers. Nonetheless I continued the sequence, if in a rather attenuated way, and I certainly enjoyed the peace of the final contemplation, resting in the moment perhaps more than most of those present. Ouch.

You might think that this experience would put me off stretching for anything, let alone for the kingdom of God. Not so. Yoga is not a violent activity, and the act of stretching is not a violent one, unlike much of the fist-clenched, macho, fight-the-good-fight approach to life which the church so often demands of those who want to follow the Prince of Peace. But as I can testify, stretching can certainly take you out of your comfort zone. Nonetheless I do not regret stretching in Grace Cathedral, and I do not regret sitting at the table of Christ and receiving the call to stretch for the kingdom from there. And there is no doubt that the repeated imagery in the epistles of the athlete-in-training has made visceral sense to me since I visited Grace Cathedral …

We are sent by God, not usually to pop a rib, but to tell others of Jesus and to struggle for justice in the world. Both these activities are stretching, and both can take you out of your comfort zone. This may be why, when all is said and done in these areas, more is said than is done. And yet to speak of Jesus and to struggle for justice are spiritual disciplines for the friends of the poor carpenter, no less so than sitting together and engaging with the endlessly interesting God. It is that God who calls us, both to speak and to struggle.

Evangelism as a spiritual practice

> Do not fear what they fear, and do not be intimidated, but in your hearts sanctify Christ as Lord. Always be ready to make your defence to anyone who demands from you an accounting for the hope that is in you; yet do it with gentleness and reverence.[4]

More people knowing Jesus. Christianity is a spacious, light, open and tolerant way, and Jesus is the shepherd, the beautiful One, and we are sent to say so. Sharing the news of the beautiful shepherd can itself be beautiful, a delicate, gentle and rich privilege. And all you need to do is talk about someone you love to someone you know. Can it really be that simple? Well, almost. You need to stretch, too.

A great deal of research has been done into the moment of sharing the faith, and the findings come down to one encouraging thing, namely that by God's grace any kind of evangelism works, provided you do it. Dwight Moody is reported to have said to one of his critics: 'It is clear you don't like my way of doing evangelism. You raise some good points. Frankly, I sometimes do not like my way of doing evangelism. But I like my way of doing it better than your way of not doing it.' And as Bishop David Pytches used to say in the context of praying for healing, 'If you don't do it, you'll never see it'.

There is a persistent myth that St Francis of Assisi once said 'Preach the Gospel; use words if necessary'. There is no recorded evidence that Francis ever did so. More than that, in the words of Archbishop Justin Welby, 'St Francis never said it – and if he ever did, he was wrong'. I agree with the Archbishop, though I think I can see why the phrase has proved so popular. There are both good and bad reasons for it.

A very good reason is that there is far more to evangelism than verbal proclamation. An example: I myself was brought to Christ as a student by two non-verbal acts.

A departure and a dance

As a teenager I had wandered away from the faith of my childhood, into the spiritual and religious marketplace of the late 1960s and early 1970s. The intellectual climate of the Acts of the Apostles, with its marketplace of gods and spiritual ways, was not that far away from the public library in Bradford and the local branch of WH Smith, which were the two places where I learned about other faiths and about things unseen. The hippy-ish ferment of the 60s had reached from Woodstock and Haight-Ashbury all the way to West Yorkshire, and I bought and borrowed books which spoke of turning on, and tuning in, and dropping out, of incantations and meditations and chants and highs, of Buddhism and Taoism and Sufism and the Order of the Golden Dawn. In short, a whole technicolour universe of the spirit was opened to me in paperback. Brightly coloured as it was, it was also dizzying. And in this spiritually dizzy state I went away to University, the first of my family ever to do so.

In 1972, away from home for the first time, in my Hall of Residence I was disturbed by a knock on the door and by the appearance of two of my fellow students 'conducting a religious survey'. They were members of the Campus Crusade for Christ.

I invited them in, since at that time I was a paperback Taoist and was happy to share my wisdom with anyone who asked. Of course it quickly transpired that the 'survey' was a ruse and that the real purpose of our conversation was for the two guys to tell me about my need for the love of Jesus. I had been a cradle Anglican and was a churchwarden's son, and at the time I recognised no such need, though I did know that they were outstaying their welcome. So, when they came to the crisis-point of their pitch and invited me to pray the 'sinner's prayer', I was very glad to do so as a way of getting rid of them. Having repeated the words given to me, admitting my sinfulness and inviting the Lord Jesus into my heart, I rather truculently asked the two guys what happened next. They stood up and said, 'We don't know. But we're leaving now; God will do the rest'. And out they went.

And that was how they evangelised me; by leaving. Nothing became their evangelism like the ending of it. I was mildly thunderstruck - not by the fact that they had left, which I greatly welcomed. The thunder that struck me was the evident belief of these young men that God had been listening to our conversation, and that God could be trusted to complete the work that they thought had been begun by the praying of the prayer. They left, and left it to God, and left me bewildered and a little shaken.

Shaken, because I think that this was the first time I had ever encountered any evidence of dependence on the living God. I cannot remember a single word of the pitch that my evangelists made, nor can I remember the words of the prayer I prayed. But the departure of these people, their belief that God was real and would get to work in their absence - this lodged in the mind, and it was enough to set the compass. I wanted what they had. From being a desperate and undifferentiated seeker for meaning and comfort, I became a seeker after truth in Christ. The Gospel was preached with words, all-too-many words; but it was heard and received in the silence of a trusting absence.

In my efforts to understand how Christians could really depend on the invisible God, I went to a number of churches. One of these was the local student church, St John's Harborne, in the charismatic/evangelical tradition of the early 1970s. I didn't have the sense to sit at the back, and so found myself within a couple of rows of the front of the church during the singing of a series of choruses. And in the middle of these songs a young woman emerged from her seat into the aisle, moved to the front of the church, and spontaneously danced her love of God. She was simply worshipping, with no intention to do evangelism or to perform. She paid no attention to the congregation, and she returned quietly to her place when the singing was done. Her dance was not particularly skilful or memorable in itself. I did not know the young woman, and as far as I know I never saw her again. But once more I was profoundly shaken, this time by beholding an offering of love to God in worship. I wanted what she had.

St Paul in 1 Corinthians, in the context of the gift of prophecy, imagines a situation similar to this: 'After the secrets of the unbeliever's heart are disclosed, that person will bow down before God and worship him, declaring, "God is really among you".' In my case my secret lostness was disclosed to me, not by prophetic words but by the demonstration of a devotion I secretly desired more than anything. And by watching this dance, I knew that the direction of my journey was confirmed.

A departure and a dance, the outworking of love and trust in God in lives lived. In the words of St Augustine of Hippo, often quoted by the Taizé community, we are to 'love, and say it with your life'.

As a bishop in conversation with Confirmation candidates I often say, in words I first heard from Church Army's Mark Russell, that 'there are five Gospels - Matthew, Mark, Luke, John and you. People will read the fifth Gospel first, and only if they find that Gospel persuasive might they open the other four'. The credibility of the Christian Way is a lived thing, life-long and life-wide, of which words are no more than a part.

'Preach the Gospel - use words if necessary'. Another argument in favour of this phrase is that faith conversations go better when they are initiated by the other person. It was Hans-Ruedi Weber in his excellent 'Experiments in Bible Study'[5] who introduced me to the centrality of 1 Peter 3:15-16 to the sharing of faith: 'In your hearts sanctify Christ as Lord. Always be ready with an explanation for anyone who asks you the grounds and shape of the hope that is within you; but do it with gentleness and respect.'[6]. Weber would share this verse with groups of people and then ask the question: who starts the conversation which is portrayed here? As often as not the automatic assumption would be that it is the Christian who begins to speak of Jesus, but of course this is not what the scripture says. It is in the answering of a question that the faith is shared, according to Peter. So using words too quickly has its disadvantages.

A third good reason is that gentleness and reverence imply reserve and reticence. Reserve can be seen as a British virtue, but in fact it's universal. In a residential conference led by John Wimber I remember hearing a guy called Danny Daniels, a big Californian pastor, an ex-rock musician, evangelical and charismatic, heavy and hairy, slow and forceful of speech, as he recounted an experience of being evangelised:

> This guy came up to me in a station and said: 'Do you know Jesus Christ as your personal Lord and Saviour?' He said it like it was one word, 'Do-you-know-Jesus-Christ-as-your-personal-Lord-and-Saviour?' I said, 'No, I don't know that. All I know is that you're very rude, talking to me without asking who I am …'[7]

A colleague of mine once used the false-Francis phrase with a local Church Council as part of a training event, sharing all of the phrase apart from one word: so - 'Preach the Gospel; use _____ if necessary'. He invited the Council members to identify the missing word. After a long pause a retired senior member of the armed services rather hesitantly said: '… use *force* if necessary?'

The general did well to be hesitant. Force would not be helpful, although of course it has been tried often enough in the long and chequered history of the Church, ranging from conversion at sword-point to simple peer-group bullying. And for many therefore, using words is just a slightly milder way of using force, and therefore is to be avoided or even resisted on the grounds of Gospel values.

It is an evident theme of this book that the Christian religion cannot, and should not, be reduced to a set of propositional tick-boxes. Life is so much more wonderful, and complicated, than that. 'Do-you-know-Jesus-Christ-as...?' - well, let's get acquainted before we make sense of that question, or of an answer to that question.

Let me see your life. Let me see the gospel you are, not just the one you proclaim. And then let's talk.

Use words

It is as we come to talk that I agree with Archbishop Justin: Indeed St Francis never said '…use words if necessary', and if he did he was wrong. On the other hand, it was the fastidious poet T. S. Eliot who wrote: 'I gotta use words when I talk to you'.[8] It is necessary at some point to use words, slippery and tricky as they are, if more people are to know Jesus. And it's necessary to use them without fear.

A bad reason for avoiding words is anxiety. The greatest single barrier to the growth of the Church is the moment of avoidance, when at the kitchen table, or at the school gate, or in the workplace or in the pub, my friend asks me what I think of something and I reply without reference to my faith, and the possibility of a moment of evangelism is lost. 'Always be ready with an explanation for anyone who asks you the grounds and shape of the hope that is within you ...' And always be ready to pay the price for offering that explanation. The price may be negligible, or it may be substantial. It may take the form of a smile or a grimace – 'I never knew you were a God-botherer'. It may take the form of a hostile conversation – 'Another f***ing religious answer'. It may simply be a lifted eyebrow, or a smile of pity. The threat and risk of any response such as these is often sufficient to stifle the conversation before it begins. And in fact, of course, the real response may have nothing to do with any of these fears. It may be neutral, or tolerant, or interested or positive or joyful or engaged. It may lead to conversation. It may lead to conversion. If you don't do it, you'll never know. If you don't do it, you'll never see it. A parallel experience comes to those who offer to pray with, or to pray for, friends in need. Whenever I have done so the effect has been positive, even on the occasions when the offer has been refused. The worst that has happened is the sort of response that goes: 'No thanks, I don't believe in that sort of thing. But thanks for asking'. The fact of goodwill offered is almost always significantly valued – far more significantly than any opinion of our friend that we are deluded to believe in the power of prayer.

So speaking up is less scary than people expect. However there is sometimes a cost, and too often Christian leaders and teachers can wind up their people to proclaim faith without in fact counting the cost. In equipping people for faith-sharing we need help and resource, because even a mild rejection can be very painful. We need help and resource from wherever it may come. And because ours is a faith fed by those on the edge of things, in the next chapter I shall speak of the great help and resource that the church can receive from the experience of LGBTI+/Queer people, within the family of God and beyond it. And I'll say that one of the many things we can learn is how to come out as a Christian, and how to overcome the anxieties that attend the moment of evangelism.

Another bad reason for avoiding words is the self-deskilling of Christian people, the sense that we are not smart enough to dare to come out as Christians, and the low self-esteem that this generates. 'If people know I'm a Christian they may ask me about why there's evil in the world, or why God allows suffering, or why the churches disagree, or why there are so many faiths, or ...'. Fear of ignorance or of appearing stupid stifles words of faith and causes the evangelistic moment to be stillborn.

Fear of not knowing the answers comes from a misunderstanding of what it is to be a witness. When I was a University student I was waiting with a friend at a bus stop. Suddenly, right in front of us, a minor road accident took place - one car shunting another, no one hurt but some damage done. My friend and I were asked to make a witness statement, and each of us duly filled in the forms provided. Just before we sent them off, we compared notes. My version of events was substantially different from his. Did this cause either of us any anxiety? No, we simply argued for a couple of good-natured moments, and then sealed the envelopes and sent our different versions off into the legal system. It was not for us to do the work of advocates. Our responsibility was to witness to what we believed we had seen, and no guilt was attached to our having seen different things.

Witnessing is a stretch, then, but not a shame-inducing one. It is in the nature of pure witnessing to be guilt-free. If God is truly God, the One who holds in being the world as it is, then the facts are friendly however unfriendly they seem, and however confused and compromised and small they make us seem in our turn. The discipline of witnessing is to express the truth of one's perception, not to tailor that perception to a pre-existing view of the world.

If I don't know why the innocent suffer, but I believe that there is a reason that's hidden from me and so I still believe in a God of love, there is no shame in saying so. Training in evangelism is not a matter of learning simplistic answers to complicated questions. It's a matter of learning how to speak the truth as I see it - that is, the whole truth from my partial perspective.

Compassion, restraint, bravery

To speak is to invite a response, and this demands a measure of courage, even if the person giving the response is a close friend or a member of your family. Evangelism is stifled whenever people prefer silence to the possibility of a negative response, and it does no good to justify that sort of silence by resorting to words which Francis of Assisi did not say, as if avoiding a truthful conversation were in some way virtuous.

Our social context does not bless the uninvited proclamation of the faith, and this is often because the faith is being proclaimed inappropriately and the culture is rightly resisting it. In the past it has been unwanted messages of judgement and damnation that have distressed people, as in the case of the ASBO given to a Christian preacher whose chosen style involved using a megaphone and shouting at people with comments such as 'You're not a winner, you're a sinner'.[9] More recently, even the explicit proclamation of life leads to trouble, as a recent news story illustrates:

> Panicked passengers forced their way out of their rush hour train after a man read out Bible passages in the carriage. The train was just outside Wimbledon at around 8.30am, when the man started reading out phrases such as 'death is not the end'... Ian, who was on the train, tweeted that the man's Bible-reading caused a 'crush' and a 'commotion'. He said that someone asked the man to stop speaking 'as he was scaring people', after which 'the guy stopped and stood there with his head down'. Other passengers praised a guard, who

apparently dealt with the situation with 'compassion, restraint and bravery.[10]

To live and profess the Christian faith is not easy or popular these days in any event. Still less is it easy to take on oneself the name of an evangelist, in a culture where 'compassion, restraint and bravery' are commended as a way of dealing with inappropriate evangelism, rather than marking the way in which evangelism itself has been done.

How then are we to share the faith? With compassion, restraint and bravery. Not seeing evangelism as the business of professional persuaders. Not justifying or excusing our own anxiety. Not learning lots of pat answers to unasked questions. Modestly, remembering always that success is not in our hands but in the hands of the One who is always beside us.

In this book I am asking what the Christian Way might look like if the image of the carpenter's table comes into the foreground. Part of this Way is the call to share faith, to engage in the moment of evangelism. That moment can be stretching certainly, but it really can also be light, spacious, natural and joyful. It is certainly an experience for all who sit at the table to share, provided the moment is grasped and not explained away, provided in this as in all things we learn from the poor Christ and from the marginalised whom he loves, provided then that the moment of 'coming out' as a Christian is supported and blessed and encouraged by those who sit at the table with us, and who long to bring others to know what it is to meet, and drink, and watch, and share.

Belonging as a spiritual way

If those who sit at the carpenter's table do indeed make room at that table for their friends, do indeed invite them to sit there and to meet the poor Christ who sits beside them, do indeed engage in the moment of evangelism, then conversations on the shape of the church can come alive. In particular there will be life in the conversations, which have been going on over many years now, about the relationship between believing, behaving and belonging as aspects of what might draw people to sit at the table as they see it laid before them.

This relationship between belief, behaviour and belonging is a subtle and complex one, which can lead to simplified and over-simplified conversations, but which is worth pursuing, if evangelism really is the purpose of it.

For a good long while the most commonly expected sequence was 'believe, behave, belong' - learn and accept the teachings of the faith, apply these teachings to your personal and social behaviour, and join the community of those who do the same. The teachings of the faith were historical (perhaps the life and teaching of Jesus, or the missionary journeys of St Paul as mapped in the appendix to so many Bibles) as well as liturgical and ethical. This way of seeing Christian life suits Christendom well. Christendom for me implies both a social reality and a social mindset. The reality, which is what we had in my own childhood, was that a large number of people embraced the 'we're all basically Christian' narrative, whether or not this translated into their own spiritual practice, as the way things were in the nation. Of course there was freedom to opt out into other faiths or no faith, and in my lifetime there has been no social cost to pay for such an opting out. But opting out was the operative process. Even more specifically, people were 'C of E' unless they told you differently.

This way of seeing society still obtains in a fast-diminishing part of our complicated England. It is strongest by definition in exactly that part of our nation and our culture where the church is strongest, and in my experience, it is most strongly defended in the church's conversations by those who live in those parts too.

In Christendom, the unexamined 'Christian' society, believing and behaving will not be seen separately. Belonging as such will not matter much. The moment of evangelism will be downplayed, because it will be assumed that we're all Christians really. The moment will take place in the world, certainly, but elsewhere; usually in the global South, among the heathen. A thoughtful Christendom church will raise money to pay other people to engage in that moment there. The focus for doctrinal teaching at home will be on the young, who will be able to learn the reasons for acting in certain ways at the same time as the ways themselves are received and accepted, at least in principle.

This way of teaching and learning formed me, and I am enormously grateful for it. And yet in my own lifetime I have seen it demolished without hope of rebuilding.

Christendom and hypocrisy

I believe that Christendom, the generally-held assumption that ours is a Christian nation and that the teachings of the Christian faith constitute the default formation for citizens, has gone over the course of my lifetime. So my father was a churchwarden and a Sunday school teacher, and in Bradford in the late 1950s and early 1960s I attended church twice each Sunday, morning and evening, and Sunday school each Sunday afternoon. At Sunday school I encountered a fair number of children whose parents did not attend church but who wanted their kids to be socialised in the Christian way. Earning a bible-story sticker for one's book by retelling the story accurately, learning to pronounce 'Quinquagesima' (or learning not to giggle at 'Sexagesima'), and committing oneself to a life of holiness were inextricably mixed together.

Literally the only thing I can remember from my confirmation preparation as a twelve-year-old was to view the service of Matins as a sequence of three rooms; a small and shadowy purple room (the penitential beginning of the service), a large and well-lit yellow room (the ministry of the word, both read and preached), and a medium-sized, calm, green room (the prayers and intercessions). And although my confirmation class teachers would have been disappointed that I had remembered so little, they would at least have been glad that their liturgical imagery has kept its place in my mind after fifty-two years. They would have seen no disconnection between communicating insight into the prayers of the church on the one hand, and teaching ethical standards on the other.

But now, a fork in the road has sundered believing and behaving. Believing itself has been privatised out of sight. This radical privatisation of faith is superbly caught in the middle of a comic monologue, I think by Jenny Eclair:

> ...He said, Is the Pope a Catholic? I said, Don't change the subject. Anyway, it's up to him what he is, innit?

In such a world, for people outside the community of faith, the social distinctiveness of believers is not what they distinctively believe, but how distinctively they act.

So for many outside the churches the sequence is now seen as 'behave, believe, belong'. Put your life straight, conform to the codes of behaviour of the community, receive instruction and catechesis in the reasons why you need to do so, and you will be accepted by God as a faithful servant and by the Christian community as a member. This way of seeing the community has a clarity which attracts some within the family of faith also, and there is an interesting alliance between those who deplore the behavioural demands of membership and those who rejoice in them. On this view, whether or not people approve of it, the common image is of a hill, sometimes steep and rocky, sometimes green and beautiful, always rising. The hill-path leads onward and upward to holiness, backward and downward to perdition. On this view to identify with the Christian family is to commit to being a climber; either that, or to being a hypocrite.

Presenting a snakes-and-ladders view of Christianity that begins with behaviour can have unforeseen consequences. Some years ago I was involved in the national Weddings Project. This was an initiative designed to analyse and address the reasons for the decline in the number of couples coming to the church for their wedding. There were plenty of anecdotal reasons which people within the church told each other to explain this trend. Perhaps it was that people no longer valued marriage, or that the wedding marketplace provided better offers, or that people had ceased to be spiritually serious. However when the Project took the unusual step of actually asking people why they had not chosen church for their wedding, the reasons were more surprising. The research was conducted by secular agencies unconnected institutionally with the church, so as to increase the chance of honest answers. Overwhelmingly people were found still to see marriage as the 'gold standard' for their relationship - far more important for example than taking out a mortgage together, or even than having a child together. And the research found high levels of spiritual seriousness among those interviewed. Yet nonetheless, of all those who saw church as the 'proper place' for their wedding, only about half actually had, or would, approach their church to discuss possibilities. And a very significant reason given was that people did not want to be, or seem to be, 'hypocritical'.

Hypocrisy is a charge frequently laid against church people; but the Weddings Project research showed that large numbers of couples, non-church people were disqualifying themselves from a church wedding. They were doing so because they assumed that they did not meet the behavioural threshold required for church connection, and therefore that they would have to be hypocritical in order to walk down the aisle. And they were not prepared to abuse what they assumed to be the conditional welcome of the church by pretending to meet the conditions. The perceived behavioural threshold was too high. Opportunities to share the beliefs of the Christian community, for example the accepting love of God, the transformative power of the Holy Spirit, the life-shaping work of repentance, alignment with Christ, friendship and ministry - all these opportunities were being lost. And lost not because of the hypocrisy of the unchurched, but precisely because the unchurched did not want to be hypocrites.

These findings of the Weddings Project chime with a more general sense that the churches are putting the cart before the horse in being seen to emphasise and demand behavioural change as a condition of faith and belonging. The reaction, as articulated especially in the so-called emerging church, was to shuffle the order of things and to invite people to 'belong, believe, behave'. It seems to me that this way of seeing things chimes with the image of the table of the poor Christ.

Sitting at the table and conversion

Earlier I said that the pattern of holiness and sanctification begins at the table: friendship – repentance – ministry. If this is so, then inviting people first to the friendship of the table and inviting them to learn the language of the faith will be the royal road to their conversion to Christ.

In a church ordered in this way - and many church plants and missional innovations are ordered in this way - the doors of the church community are open to all, and no one needs to disqualify themselves on the grounds of an insufficient conformity. Such a church will say to all, 'You are welcome as you are morally and behaviourally, and we have no problem with you staying where you are for a while, even a very long while, so long as you are happy to remain in touch with God's people'. This strategy implies faith in the transforming power of the Spirit. The assumption is that the work of grace in a visitor's heart will in the end persuade them of the truth of the faith, and will in the end conform their behaviour and ways of life to the values and pattern of Jesus.

This is by no means a modern invention.

> 'When William Penn was convinced of the principles of Friends, and became a frequent attendant at their meetings, he did not immediately relinquish his gay apparel; it is even said that he wore a sword, as was then customary among men of rank and fashion . Being one day in company with George Fox, he asked his advice concerning it, saying that he might, perhaps, appear singular among Friends, but his sword had once been the means of saving his life without injuring his antagonist, and moreover, that Christ has said, 'he that hath no sword, let him sell his garment and buy one.' George Fox answered, 'I advise thee to wear it as long as thou canst.' Not long after this they met again, when William had no sword, and George said to him, 'William, where is thy sword?' 'Oh!' said he, I have taken thy advice; I wore it as long as I could.'[11]

This charming story is historically unfounded. But although it is not factual, it is too good not to be true. In it among other things it's interesting to see that William Penn, who was perhaps already living in bad faith, had found a scriptural proof-text as well as a social excuse to justify his sword-wearing. But in the end the quality of life of the Quaker community overcame his selective reading of the Bible, without as it seems the need for exhortation or other pressure on the part of George Fox or anyone else.

Early Quakerism was a missional movement, and large numbers of pioneer ministers and others before and since have found this sequence to be refreshing and fruitful, as well as deeply contentious. In particular the unredeemed personal and sexual lives of new converts regularly leads to trouble, as personal and sexual behaviour incessantly does in the life of the churches. These Anabaptist church planters from the old East Germany (the GDR) speak for many:

> It was not uncommon for couples in Halle to be unwed, but cohabit and have children together. We were faced with a dilemma of couples in this situation who were becoming interested in following Jesus and yet had many negative stereotypes of marriage. As church leaders, we struggled knowing when to ask these couples to get married. Should we tell them to get separate apartments or to sleep separately if they were not ready to get married? How much pressure should we put on them to marry, and what consequences would we set if they chose not to marry? Instead of focusing on setting policies or thinking up consequences, we kept loving them and talking with them about God's intentions for marriage. Eventually they came to realize that it was a next step in their faith journey to marry and those weddings were always a highlight in the life of the church. But in the meantime, it was messy explaining to other Christians that we had unmarried couples living together in our church for significant lengths of time.
>
> While we rejoiced … and learned to love and worship with unwed couples, we learned that people who had been Christians for many years as an adult had the most problem with the messiness of our church since that is not what they were used to. The people most happy with our approach were those who had no church background and were positively surprised by 'church' not looking like the negative propaganda they had been exposed to in the days of the GDR.[12]

This is the church of the table; inclusive and messy in its nature. Indeed 'messiness' is a word commonly used of this way of being the church. It both describes and conceals a worry; that those who prefer to see behaviour transformed before acceptance is offered are right, and that in its messiness the community is refusing holiness and is indeed betraying the gospel. I am relaxed about these worries. If God is real, then the work of God's Spirit will not need border guards. 'Belong, believe, behave' has been a fruitful sequence for the missional; fruitful I would say for all who commit themselves to sitting beside the poor Christ at the carpenter's table and to extending the table into every street and every home. It privileges openness and hospitality and it makes room for ambiguity, and for all the things that being human will bring. It is courteous, gracious, and respectful of the material with which God is working, that is with the humanity of the human. It does not in fact imply doctrinal or behavioural laxity, but it does demand patience of its practitioners; the willingness for them daily to be transformed into the image of the poor Christ, and the willingness constantly to be surprised by what that image may be, and where it may lead them to stand.

Guests and hosts

In any case, whose table is it? Whose church is it?

When I was a Team Vicar, 25 years ago or so, my church had a car park. Arriving at church on my day off one day I found a man parked in a reserved spot. I pointed this out to him, and his not-unexpected response was 'And who the blazes are you?' My profoundly inaccurate and unchristian reply? 'Listen, you. I'm the Vicar here. I own this church.' As soon as I said it I winced. And I remembered some words of missioner and church planter Kerry Thorpe: 'Jesus said, "I will build my church". He made no promise about anybody else's.'

'I own this church'? Oh, my goodness.

The proprietary attitude of Christian people towards the gifts that God has given us is off-putting, to say the least. Grumpy vicars in car parks are joined by regiments of Christians, ordained and lay, who erect barriers and walls and fences around the extraordinary gift of grace that is the friendship of Jesus, and who presume then to test and examine people who seek to enter, and indeed to examine those already there, to establish whether they are 'worthy' to remain. Oh. My. Goodness.

Well, the penalty fits the crime. If you want a small, pure church badly enough, you will certainly get what you want. But be careful what you ask for. It can be lonely, being right about everything. In my Yorkshire youth I was told the story of the man who said to his friend, 'The whole world's crooked except for me and thee. And I'm none too sure about thee'.

By contrast Jesus seems to have welcomed, and sat beside, just about anyone. It's true that he had a problem with hypocrites and professionally pious writers and legalistic types. But he went to eat, even with them.

Much is said today, and rightly so, about the need for God's people to be radically hospitable, and to open the door in welcome to those on the edge of things. I stand by this approach and, as you will have noticed, I spend much of my time advocating for it.

But for the Church to talk of hospitality and welcome can be misleading.

As a bishop I do not own the house I live in. When I go to church I will not own that building either. Nor will I own the imposing and uncomfortable chair which will be offered me to sit in. Most of all I do not own the table at which I will celebrate Communion. It is not my table. It is the Lord's table. It is not my church, but Jesus' church – he who said 'I will build my church', but who made no promise about anybody else's.

So it is not for me to welcome people to Jesus' table, except in the sense that an early guest at a party opens the door to later guests to make sure they can get in. I need to know my place.

And yet even this is not quite right.

Because in his life on earth among us, Jesus didn't own any tables either. He has built one since, by his Spirit, and we can all sit at it and be welcome, and eat the bread of heaven there. But in his years of ministry on the earth he had nowhere to lay his head. Whenever he sat to eat, it was as a guest at someone else's table. Zacchaeus, Simon the Pharisee, Mary and Martha, that unnamed person who lent his upper room – they were the hosts.

And Jesus was always a guest, by his own choice.

A guest has no right to fence the table and to say who the other guests will be. A guest shares, and speaks, and listens, and eats, with courtesy and in gratitude. A guest is not in the middle and at the top, but on the edge and underneath. From that place a guest may hear the words of the host, 'Friend, come and sit up here'.

And it is as a guest that Jesus – and his Church – does mission.

The late Bishop John V. Taylor of Winchester used to speak of christening services in this way: *'The family invites us, the Church, to its baptism service. They are the hosts and we attend as guests with our gifts. We* are welcome there, and the family are glad when we unwrap our gifts – the gift of the promise of life eternal, the gift of inclusion in the church family, the gift of sharing in God's word and God's life. But we do not welcome them. They welcome us. Approach things in this way, and you will be welcome.'

So I try to approach things in this way.

Whose table is it? Not mine, certainly. Not even Jesus', since he chose to sit as a guest.

It's the table of the people I meet, the ones I serve and the ones God loves; and I sit there at their invitation, and from there I share what I have been given, when I'm asked. I speak the name of Jesus the guest, as a guest. And as a guest I invite my hosts to sit at another table where I'm a guest, the table where the Carpenter is the host, the table of the poor man, the table of the King.

More justice in the world

... a bruised reed he will not break, and a smouldering wick he will not quench, until he brings justice to victory; and in his name the Gentiles will hope.[1]

Draw a line that includes us and excludes many others, and Jesus Christ is always on the other side of the line. At least that is so if we are speaking of the biblical, historic Christ who eats with sinners and outsiders, who is made a curse and sin itself for us, who justifies the ungodly, and who is himself the hole in any system.[2]

On giants' shoulders

Present and future bishops of Liverpool are very much aware of standing on giants' shoulders. The sixth bishop (David Sheppard, bishop 1975-1998) and the seventh (James Jones, bishop 1999-2013) each made an enormous regional and national impact for the common good. From *Faith in the City* to the Hillsborough Independent Panel, the role of the Church and its leaders has been maximised by these men in the service of a prophetic vision of the Kingdom of God. When Bishop James was asked to give very substantial time to the chairing of the Hillsborough Independent Panel he accepted the challenge, because the injustice and frustration and agony that had been visited on the Hillsborough families needed to be seriously and sacrificially addressed, as a Gospel matter. And in his rigorous and faithful work over the years, he commended the

Christian religion afresh in his generation as a serious contributor to the transformation of the world.

This sort of work is not painless. Bishop David in particular became a figure of contention in his day, deeply unpopular among many, because of the views he held and the stands he took. Much of England, though by definition not a voting majority, faces in a different direction from the one implemented in the policies of the last few governments. Certainly this is true of my part of Merseyside, where the Conservative party and the Liberal Democrats are very thinly represented in the national or regional leadership. In such a context the pastorally-based political witness of David Sheppard and his friend Archbishop Derek Worlock rang a true note for the people of the region and in particular for the people of the city of Liverpool. They were loved and are remembered because they spoke for those with no voice.

Worlock wrote their manifesto in a sense, when in 1995 he composed for Sheppard a parody of the folk-song 'In My Liverpool Home'. Someone worked it into a cross-stitch sampler, and Bishop David's daughter gave the sampler to me. It hangs on the wall at the entrance to the bishop's chapel today:

> In our Liverpool home,
> Sent here from Lambeth and Rome,
> We're better together in protest and prayer,
> We've shouted for jobs in a voice loud and clear,
> When the city wants allies we're proud to be here,
> In our Liverpool home.

Here were two men, each born to privilege and of high ability, prepared for the sake of their faith to take public stands which made them unpopular with their own peer groups, 'traitors to their class' if you like. Cheap accusations of Marxism were regularly thrown at them, and they were condemned as unspiritual and political prelates, unfaithful to Jesus, with no time for the proper business of religion. Their own self-understanding was simply that they were standing (or as I would say sitting) alongside the poor Christ, who was sharply visible to them in the unemployed poor and in the socially disadvantaged. The credibility they won for the churches flowed from this commitment to justice.

Do justly

So when in today's Diocese of Liverpool we say that we are asking God for a bigger church so as to make a bigger difference, 'more people knowing Jesus, *more justice in the world*', it is these examples that we remember, and this tradition that we try to inhabit. And in my personal witness the question has been, what must I do, what must we do, in our generation to sit beside these giants at the table, and from there to look in the direction they looked, and to challenge the injustice we see as they challenged what they saw, and to advocate for justice as they advocated for it?

One answer is straightforward; we are to look where they looked and to sustain the witness they pioneered. We are to defend those who are increasingly disadvantaged by years of 'austerity', and who are intimidated and bewildered by the ever-changing systems of benefit claims. We are to stand with those who have been decanted by the refugee and asylum-seeker systems into the North-West of England and left to negotiate their way through the mazes and minefields of legal process. We are to defend and help all those who are increasingly hungry – physically hungry – and must simply be fed, and strengthened. We are to stand beside local leaders of all faiths and of none, as they struggle to care for their people while facing drastic cuts to their budgets in the past few years. We are to stand beside them (as Worlock said) in protest and prayer. We are to maintain pastoral care for those whose loved ones were killed at Hillsborough or in any other violent and unjust context, and to open space for them to grieve, and to sit alongside them in their anger and hope.

All this I see as pointing to the pastoral concern that contributes to the transformation of the world. In Liverpool we stretch for the kingdom of justice and peace, alongside tens of thousands of Christians across the nation and millions across the worlds who stretch for the same future, and we seek with God's help to bring it in. I believe that the struggle for justice is a foundation of discipleship. And so anyone sitting at the table alongside the poor carpenter will be challenged to stretch for a just future.

What must we do in our generation? A further answer is to learn from the witness of the quite recent past, especially where that witness has already been lost or eroded or ignored. One aspect of that witness for example, evident in *Faith in the City*, is the passionate desire not only to help the poor but to learn from their wisdom and humour and courage, to sit alongside, to shut up and listen. 'Faith in the City' was eloquent on this, rejecting once and for all the lady-bountiful image of social witness, seeking to do good without ever being do-gooders:

> There is no reason to think that the Gospel is more authentically lived out in 'comfortable Britain' ... Our task as a church is by no means only to show concern for the victims of oppressive social conditions; it is also to find ways of discerning and receiving the gifts of those who have worked out a genuine Christian discipleship under circumstances of 'multiple deprivation'.[3]

I feel acutely the challenge of these words, as I look at my own history and at the Church I am helping to shape today. The leadership of today's Church at every level still demands and depends on a skill-set in managing complex language and concept, a skill-set which raises insuperable barriers to millions of English people and hundreds of thousands of English Christian disciples. This is true across the landscape of our internal conversations about the best way to be the church in these days. It is true irrespective of whether people prefer to advocate for 'good management' or 'good theology'. The air we breathe and the language we speak is academic or quasi-academic by default; expensive, elitist, class-ridden, ineluctably exclusive. Learning to breathe that air and speak that language has caused me too to be a traitor to my class, I who am the son of a works manager and a home-help supervisor. I am a beneficiary of this academic system, and of course I see and celebrate its value and its qualities. I could not have written this book without the gifts of my education to me. I neither regret nor repent of those gifts, of the education I was freely given by the church and the state. But I deeply regret that it has established norms that exclude so many, and it angers and shames me that those who do not share these norms are still excluded from the ministries of the church as a matter of routine.

My episcopal neighbour and brother Bishop Philip North of Burnley speaks eloquently and accurately of the selective and biased way we select and train our ministers, and of the way our methods expect people to be at ease in what he calls an 'officer-training' context. Theology is now done in ways which would disqualify most (if not all) of the people our Lord called to be with him at the first tables of our community. Over thirty years ago, at the same time as the Doctrine Commission was doing its thinking in the ways I described in an earlier chapter, the *Faith in the City* Commission was advocating for a greater inclusion, in words which seem to me to have become even more urgent:

> … truths which are really important to us are not conveyed and received only through sets of logically related propositions, and there is no obvious necessity to give this kind of thinking priority over other means of communication which God may use to stir our imagination and bend our will to his purpose. (We are forced) to ask whether theology must always have such an academic character if it is to be authentic.[4]

I try to do justice, then, by remembering what my forebears have said about these things. And I try in a third way also; I try to identify those on the edge today, those from whom we may learn today, those whose voice has been stolen from them today.

Wisdom from the edge of things

The moral agonies of the world at the time of writing, agonies in which of course the churches as human institutions are fully implicated, include the routine oppression and objectification of women, the enormous difficulty for institutions and individuals of 'getting' the need for a fully just process of safeguarding, the constant and in some places increasing need for racial justice and sexual and gender justice, and (I write these words in the United States) the need for children to grow up unafraid either of being targeted by gunfire or caught in crossfire. All these matters are alive and pressing, and to aim for more justice in the world is to be unable to ignore them, since the world we speak of is the world God loved so much that God's only Son was given for it.

And the Church, living as it does immersed in history, and with its own dynamic and its own history, does not get to choose the issues on which it needs to make its choices and to take its stands. To the irritation and embarrassment of many in the churches, human sexuality remains a matter of deep contention for us, further complicated as the nations of the West change their views radically around us.

I write as an Anglican/Episcopalian bishop within a diverse and relational church. I believe that I am called by God to advocate and to persuade for justice as I see it, but not unilaterally to prescribe. Ours is not a command economy. So I cannot prescribe for other Christians the position they must take on, for example, the inclusion of LGBTI+ people in the life of the church and the eradication of homophobia from church and nation alike. But I will certainly advocate for a stand, the stand that I believe should be taken on these matters. The struggle for inclusion and the struggle against homophobia are matters which, as I see them, cannot be separated. And as the great Jesuit activist and theologian and poet Daniel Berrigan said, it is good in this matter as in any other to 'know where you stand – and stand there'.

And surely for any Christian the process is the same; to meet at the table and drink from the fountain and watch in the moment so as to be close to the poor carpenter who died for us, and in his name to be close to those who for whatever reason are pushed to the edge of things, and who suffer there.

Despised and rejected

> We must be saved together.
> We cannot go to God alone;
> else He would ask
> 'Where are the others?'[5]

The letter to Philippians is a joyful and confident communication, despite its unpropitious context. It is written from prison and out of privation. But it's full of delight in the work of God which cannot be bound in prison; full of joy in the companionship which the writer has received through membership of the church. It evidences a calm readiness to see the good news of Jesus spread, even rejoicing in the work of those whose motives and actions have hurt the writer. From this balanced and joyful spirit, unbowed by imprisonment, comes a description of the work of the Lord Jesus which has inspired and focused the thinking of many over the centuries, and which has gathered still greater influence in the churches more recently. It is utterly central to my own understanding of the person and work of Christ. It comes in the form of a poem, perhaps sung as a hymn.

> Adopt the attitude that was in Christ Jesus:
> Though he was in the form of God,
> he did not consider being equal with God something to exploit.
> But he emptied himself
> by taking the form of a slave
> and by becoming like human beings.
> When he found himself in the form of a human,
> he humbled himself by becoming obedient to the point of
>   death,
> even death on a cross.
>
> Therefore, God highly honoured him
> and gave him a name above all names,
> so that at the name of Jesus everyone
> in heaven, on earth, and under the earth might bow
> and every tongue confess that
> Jesus Christ is Lord, to the glory of God the Father.[6]

Through the eyes of faith, the One who emptied himself is the limitlessly strong and powerful One of Revelation, and at the same time is the One that Isaiah saw, the One who does not break the fragile body, or extinguish the guttering flame of a person's spirit, until justice comes to victory. It is this One who 'emptied himself…'

The Greek word '*kenos*' means empty. Its verb '*kenoō*' means to make empty, to nullify, to be made desolate, to come to nothing.[7] On the face of it this is not a very encouraging cluster of meanings. The word is only used of Jesus in this one passage in the Bible. Its use makes clear that the exaltation of Jesus as the One before whom all shall bow depends on his emptying, his nullification, his desolation, his reduction to nothingness. And from its use has emerged a model for Christian living, and self-understanding, which is radically subversive of human exaltation, defensiveness, exceptionalism and arrogant pride. In his angular and profound translation of Philippians, David Bentley Hart catches the place of the cross at the heart of this emptying:

> He emptied himself, taking a slave's form, coming to be in a likeness of human beings; and, being found as a human being in shape, He reduced himself, coming obedient all the way to death, and a death by a cross.[8]

Steeped in this scripture and in a lifetime's reflection on the Cross, my great spiritual father and guide Roland Walls said this: 'Success, in the Christian enterprise, has to pass through this lonely man, Jesus, who failed completely'.[9]

To follow Jesus is to follow him in this self-emptying. When I speak of watching with the poor carpenter in the moment, I speak of this emptiness as it comes to us in our awareness and in our prayer. And when I speak of stretching for the kingdom of the carpenter, I speak of the identification of Christians with our empty and desolate Lord who has nowhere to lay his head, and so with those who are themselves – for whatever reason – empty and desolate and on the edge of things.

When we read Philippians 2, familiarity may jump us too quickly from the emptiness to the exaltation, just as each Holy Week we may jump too quickly from Good Friday to Easter Day. Martin Luther had a hard word for his own church and ours on this matter. He wrote: 'Nevertheless, the dear, pleasure-loving world goes merrily along, takes none of this (the abandonment of the crucified Lord) to heart, is lazy, cold, unthankful, and despises this great treasure.[10]'

But the treasure is there for anyone to find who seeks. Jesus teaches us what we need to know about our disposition to the world by means of his emptiness and desolation. Our own exaltation as beloved children is utterly certain, but we are not called to luxuriate in that certainty if the complacent result is that our eyes drift over the empty and desolate, on our streets and sitting beside us in our churches.

This empty and desolate Christ is the One of whom Isaiah wrote, who said:

> He grew up like a young plant before us,
> like a root from dry ground.
> He possessed no splendid form for us to see,
> no desirable appearance.
> He was despised and avoided by others;
> a man who suffered, who knew sickness well.
> Like someone from whom people hid their faces,
> he was despised, and we didn't think about him.
>
> It was certainly our sickness that he carried,
> and our sufferings that he bore,
> but we thought him afflicted,
> struck down by God and tormented.
> He was pierced because of our rebellions
> and crushed because of our crimes.
> He bore the punishment that made us whole;
> by his wounds we are healed.
>
> Like sheep we had all wandered away,
> each going its own way,
> but the Lord let fall on him all our crimes.[11]

Not only the poor carpenter but the despised and wounded Servant sits beside us at the table. It is the table that the Servant made, who asks us to notice and learn from the despised and wounded here and now. The call to do so comes to us from the living Christ, through the scripture and through the concerns of the world God loves and which God has given to us as our field and our care.

Queer Virtue[12]

In each generation the empty and desolate Christ forces on the churches the needs and the proper demands of his colleagues and companions, the empty and desolate children of God. Ours is no exception.

So in the United States where I have written this book, the running sore of unreconciled racism is a matter with which the churches struggle daily, and though God knows there is a long way to go, the churches I met are engaging in this struggle more courageously and more effectively than the (in every sense) established churches of the UK.

Other issues of justice include the real, and not the token, inclusion of women in the common life of the churches. They include the righteous claims of black, Asian and minority ethnic people to be seen and heard and their strong and proper assertion that their lives matter. They include the proper claims for justice of those children and vulnerable adults, who have been abused by their fellow Christians and in particular by the leaders of the churches. Each and all of these issues cast dark shadows on the table of the carpenter, but that table can bear the shadows because the One who built it was acquainted with sorrow and grief, with emptiness and desolation.

But among all these voices, I myself have felt called, by the God who brings wisdom from the edge of things, to notice and learn from specific groups today, and in particular those who have been pushed to the edge because of their sexuality, and/or because they do not fit a simplistic binary understanding of what it is to be a human person.

LGBTI+/Queer inclusion has not been the gladly chosen and agreed agenda of the churches in my generation. But it is one which the world God loves has presented to the churches, and in particular the churches of the West. And I want to notice and learn from my queer and LGBTI+ friends – absolutely not to patronise or diminish these proud children of God, but to understand through the lens of their experience how far my own life has been diminished by the false consciousness that always comes from ignoring those on the edge of things.

In the US, from where I write these words, the conversation around the full inclusion of LGBTI+ people in the life of God's people has been more honestly and more radically explored, just as the racism of the churches has been more fully explored. Many of the churches, including the Episcopal Church, have corporately entered the place of emptiness and desolation, in which LGBTI+ people have lived and still live, with a view to learning from the wisdom of the wounded, finding the word and love of Christ there.

And I am clear that any church that stands with those who have been made empty and desolate, with all the contentious and fractious consequences that come from standing there, will find the nourishment that the One who took the form of a slave gives to those who sit at his battered and splintered table with his friends.

People on the edge of things are not problems, and emptiness and desolation do not last forever. The table is indeed battered and splintered, but a commonly-heard sound there is laughter, and joy is a common experience. As Liz Edman says, 'That's part of what the church is missing out on; the joy of queer people, people of color, etc. I tend to think the church needs more joy across the board, but that's a bigger project!'

Anyway, I have learned courage and delight from people pushed to the edge, and so among other things I have chosen in my own ministry to speak for the greater inclusion of LGBTI+ people in the life of the churches. As I do so I have had people say to me, 'For goodness' sake stop going on about these things and concentrate on the gospel'. I have been reminded of the words of Malcolm Muggeridge, who many decades ago said of the churches, 'they have sex on the brain, which is the worst possible place to have it'. I have been invited to turn my attention from temporal things and to concentrate on the eternal. I have been called a false teacher, and people have refused to receive Communion from my hands. I have been richly and personally abused by a crowd of people whom I do not know.

I am unshaken and unpersuaded by any of this. The love of Christ constrains me, and the Christ whose love constrains me is the empty and desolate and joyful One, and so I will exhort myself and my friends to include all at the table, to lay down our carefully-constructed purities and our painfully-evident superiorities. I will exhort us to do this, not so that we can be trendy and liberal and blithely heretical, but for the sake of the despised and broken Christ, and for the quality of our prayers and the salvation of our immortal souls.

In the deeply profound words of Max Warren, 'It takes a whole world to know the whole Gospel' – the whole of the world, and a world that is whole. If Christians assume that those who are different are less than whole, are sick and must be cured, then we miss the desolate Christ within, projecting our own brokenness on to the different and blaming them for being who they are, not seeing that our love for God can only be as great as our love for the person we love least. Martin Buber says this better in a Hasidic story, where the tzaddik (the holy teacher) is asked, 'Why can we no longer see the face of God?', and answers, 'Because we have forgotten how to stoop so low'.[13]

Pride

Our anxious churches, so keen to grow or else to survive uncorrupted, specifically need to embrace the witness of the excluded if they are to be whole. The alternative way is the way of Midas; wealth and gold everywhere, and no life. To label the different as if with the label 'Biohazard' and to exclude them from our fellowship is to turn away from life. To choose sameness is to enter a desert of the spirit, where the carpets are luxurious and the chuckles and in-jokes fall like snow, where money and like-minded heartiness flows from the fountains, and where the soul dies for want of living water. Against all this the voice that witnesses to life at the table is the voice of the different One, the marginal and empty and joyous and living One, who leaps the barriers of our sameness and speaks wisdom from beyond the walls. And in these days, one place to seek that voice of wisdom is among the queer.

In her fine book *Queer Virtue* Liz Edman writes of the richness and nourishment that can come to the churches from the experience of queer people in negotiating and living their lives in emptiness and desolation, and in finding honour and Pride in who they are, and (if they are Christians) in giving praise to Jesus Christ who shared their emptiness and desolation and who shared with them his exaltation.

Liz speaks of Pride not as the arrogance I mentioned above, a deadly sin, but as the virtue of self-acceptance in Christ and the overcoming of an externally taught self-loathing. She sees the distinction clearly. She says:

> Cultivating Pride is tricky for Christians because we must embrace our value as children of God while simultaneously rejecting all the triumphalist, militaristic, hubristic crap that still pervades our tradition. If you grew up singing 'Onward

Christian Soldiers' practically every other week in church, you know how hard this is. We have to be queering those imperialistic interpretations and tendencies, constantly. If we are going to 'Lift high the Cross', we need to be very clear; it's not an act of conquest, nor a proclamation of superiority to others … Lifting up the cross is a way of saying that we aren't afraid of love. Standing there, knowing the violence that gets directed at love, we affirm the Christian premise that although our bodies may be killed, our souls cannot die.[14]

'Pride' in this sense, the recovery of self-esteem in a context of God's gracious and freely-bestowed esteem, and of self-acceptance in a context of God's clear 'yes', is one of the ways in which those on the margins can bring wisdom to the heart of us all. In an era when the Christian faith has become a 'toxic brand' for so many, every Christian needs to recover the moment of Pride in being who we are in God, and to distinguish it from the arrogance with which our witness has so often been marked in the past. Those who sit at the table at the invitation of the empty and desolate One have no reason to be proud, and every reason to receive Pride as a gift of grace from the One who is now exalted.

It was with this understanding of Pride that I was privileged and honoured to become a Patron of Liverpool Pride, and deeply humbled to be accepted and included in the Pride community more widely. This was not an uncontroversial step for me. Some who disapproved of my involvement with Liverpool Pride wrote to me in sorrow, and more wrote in anger. The general sense of these communications was that I had made a mistake in conferring 'legitimacy' or 'recognition' on the LGBTI+ community by associating with the Pride events.

My own perspective was diametrically different from this. As I saw it, it was the LGBTI+ community which had conferred the honour of recognition on me, a representative of so much that had hurt and still hurts its people. Far from wanting to remind me of these millions of hurtful moments, my new friends and colleagues at Pride were unconditional in their acceptance and enthusiastic in their affirmation of a Christian (one of many on the event) who simply wanted to walk with the community and to affirm God's love for its people. It was by this acceptance and affirmation that the gift of the poor Christ was given to me on that day.

And I responded in repentance for all that I and my community had done to demean and distress LGBTI+ human beings. I was able to speak with and share with and offer help to people on that day and subsequently. In short, through my involvement with Liverpool Pride I experienced life-changing friendship leading to repentance and ministry; the classic pattern of those who meet and sit at the carpenter's table, as described at length elsewhere in this book.

I am human, and so I am as much in need of repentance, as broken and as sinful, as other members of the straight community, or as members of the LGBTI+/Queer community. But this is a function of our shared humanity, not of my or their orientation, and certainly not a result of anyone's deep desire to express their love for the ones they love. In a speech in our General Synod I was glad to be able to say that LGBTI+ orientation and identity is not a crime, not a sickness and not a sin. And I am privileged to know LGBTI+ people who in their lives have been treated as criminals or sick people or sinners and who have nonetheless come to a place of Pride in the face of all rejection, by the grace of the empty and desolate Christ and in the power of the Spirit. There is a Spirit they feel that delights to do no evil. I want to learn from them how to be a Christian.

Coming out Christian

Another gift of the LGBTI+ community to the Christian family, which Liz Edman underlines in her book, is the experience of coming out - of declaring the truth about yourself to those who know you, with Pride but also with due acknowledgement that the moment isn't always an easy one. Indeed it has been and still is deeply painful for many. The legalisation of same-sex marriage and the growing levels of inclusion in Western society are good things but they are not sufficient to shield LGBTI+ people from pain or severe stress. On the day I wrote this the Guardian newspaper carried an article on the continuing high incidence of self-loathing in the LGBTI+ community, together with the news item that

Bermuda had repealed its same-sex marriage legislation with the assent of the UK government.

In such a context, of course coming out remains difficult, and often more difficult in the context of Christian faith. Over the decades the LGBTI+ community has built a body of wisdom on this moment of truth, and on how best to support and nurture those who face that moment and courageously enter it. What Liz has done is to recognise that the learning that comes from this can help to equip all Christians for the moment of evangelism - that is, the moment of 'coming out' as a Christian.

As I said in the last chapter, there is no doubt that coming out as a Christian can be hard, and that in some contexts it can invite painful rejection. I do not in any way equate this response with the infinitely more stressful and existential rejection felt by so many LGBTI+ people at the point of coming out. My point is that in this as in so much, we can learn from those on the edge of things. The body of hard-won wisdom on coming out in the LGBTI+ context can offer sound teaching to those who teach and commend evangelism in the churches, and in particular I write this for the attention of my friends in progressive/liberal churches. As Liz Edman writes:

> Christians talk about the importance of witnessing to our faith. But how do we do this? There is arguably not a single aspect of Christianity that so completely eludes progressive church members ... Little wonder that the progressive Christian footprint in the collective Christian consciousness is so faint.[15]

I speak of the moment of evangelism elsewhere in this book, drawing on Liz Edman's practical thinking there. Here I simply want to underline the general point that in a faith built around the self-emptying Christ, we will not be surprised to see learning come from the edges, and that here is an exemplary case in point. To learn specifically about *evangelism* from the LGBTI+ community may seem counter-cultural for some Christians, but the learning is profound and clear, and whatever the spread of opinion may be on the expression of LGBTI+ love, the learning remains for all Christians who are prepared to receive it.

Open Table

In 2014 I spoke of the table of the poor carpenter, Jesus Christ, and of my belief that Jesus wanted that table to be extended down every street and into every home so that He might sit beside all who want to sit there. By one of those divine ironies I preached this sermon unaware of the existence of Open Table Liverpool.

Open Table is one of the congregations of our Diocese, and it is now one of many Open Tables across the UK. It aims to be open to all, but especially and explicitly to LGBTI+ people for whom a genuinely open table is a pressing need, and to whom the churches' tables have been too firmly closed or hedged for too long.

But I did know, and readers too will know because it has been said repeatedly across the Churches, that if we are to resolve our conversations around same-sex issues, then among other things we must listen closely and carefully to the experience of LGBTI+ people and among them to the experience of LGBTI+ Christians.

Listening closely and carefully to people is in itself a spiritual discipline, demanding openness and in a different sense emptiness; certainly demanding the patience not to speak too soon. Evangelists in particular need to learn it. Too often it seems easier to speak, and if necessary to shout, until people either say that they agree with us, or until the conversation ends with dust being shaken from feet. Without careful listening we're left with raw contention. And goodness knows, we are used to that. But as an evangelist, I know that if I listen closely and carefully to people, then I will draw close to the moment of conversion – not only theirs but also mine. This was Peter's experience with Cornelius.

It was with Walter Hollenweger, my professor of mission, the one-time Pentecostal pastor, the Swiss Reformed theologian and world authority on the history of Pentecostalism, that I learned the theology of mission. For him the story of Peter and Cornelius as told in Acts 10 and 11 was a formative text. He would say: 'Here we read of the conversion of Cornelius; but surely we also read of the conversion of Peter'. In the apostle's own words:

> I was in the city of Joppa praying when I had a visionary experience. In my vision, I saw something like a large linen sheet being lowered from heaven by its four corners. It came

all the way down to me. As I stared at it, wondering what it was, I saw four-legged animals—including wild beasts—as well as reptiles and wild birds. I heard a voice say, 'Get up, Peter! Kill and eat!' I responded, 'Absolutely not, Lord! Nothing impure or unclean has ever entered my mouth.' The voice from heaven spoke a second time, 'Never consider unclean what God has made pure'.[16]

Peter's vision has the authentic flavour of emptiness and desolation, as his old certainties about holiness and purity crumble. The voice of God declaring God's creation clean radically changes him. Changed as he is, he opens himself to an encounter with the gentile Cornelius and his friends. The meeting changes him further as he sees the work of the Spirit evident in them. And this brings him into immediate trouble with the Church. Let Hollenweger take up the story:

When frontiers are crossed, when new dimensions of faith are discovered – above all when this is in contradiction to hitherto dearly-held principles – it seems that quarrel in the Church is inevitable. That was already the case in the original Christian community. Quarrel belongs to the Church. That does not necessarily mean that those who quarrel have to reproach each other with dishonest motives. According to Luke's text the apostles allowed Peter to present his story. And now a very remarkable thing happens. They are won over by the facts – not by evidence from Scripture...[17]

The response of the Jerusalem community to Peter's story, which is presented by him without any reference to scriptural exegesis, is unequivocal: 'When they heard this, they were silenced. And they praised God, saying, "Then God has given even to the Gentiles the repentance that leads to life".' Hollenweger goes on:

Where did this astonishing confidence come from? 'There can only be one answer,' writes Lesslie Newbigin in discussing the commissioning of the missionaries from Antioch. 'It is because they are convinced that these new Christians have received the Spirit'. I have mentioned only a few of the difficulties in this remarkable story. However critically one might comment on it, no one can disregard the fact that it is part of the Bible

… The disturbing fact in this story is just this, that an apostle
who was called to be a rock in the Church learns something in
the course of his evangelism which he had not known before.
But, tell me, is evangelism any different today?[18]

In 2015, with this understanding of mission and evangelism in my
own DNA, I visited Open Table on its seventh birthday to celebrate
the Holy Eucharist with them. I encountered in this community the
face of the Christ of the poor. The quality of this fresh expression
of the Church struck me so forcefully that I was moved to give
them a gift, an icon portraying the Lord Jesus Christ among the
broken poor. When I gave it to the Open Table congregation, I
made clear to them that it was not their sexual orientation that I
saw as brokenness. I said that for many of their friends who lived
in this society at risk and in fear, they themselves were the face of
Christ shining.

The fact is that Open Table's Christians, like so many LGBTI+
people, have been bruised and broken by our society's response to
who they are. And of course the harsh fact is that the Church has
played, and still plays, no small part in this bruising and breaking. I
therefore felt, and still feel, the obligation to repent on behalf of my
sisters and brothers. I wanted to express my sorrow to this small and
faithful congregation for the way in which Christians had treated
them. I also wanted to express my thanks to them for continuing to
minister and evangelise in the name of Jesus Christ despite all this.

So in the midst of New York where Liz Edman ministers, and in
the midst of Liverpool where I minister, and in the midst of your
own region (because of course this is not unique to Liverpool or
New York) are congregations of LGBTI+ men and women, seeking
to follow the self-emptying Jesus Christ out of the truth of who
they are. Many of them have suffered street violence for their sexual
orientation, and some of them continue to do so. In the midst of
this pain, they have expressed the love of Jesus Christ not only to
LGBTI+ communities but also to the wider Church. And in my
attempts to give close attention to this experience, I have myself
been profoundly changed, as Peter was with Cornelius.

The Church conforms itself to Jesus Christ when it sees the face of Jesus Christ. In a famous and compelling passage, Pope Francis speaks for the self-emptying church when he says:

> I prefer a Church which is bruised, hurting and dirty because it has been out on the streets, rather than a Church which is unhealthy from being confined and from clinging to its own security. I do not want a Church concerned with being at the centre and which then ends by being caught up in a web of obsessions and procedures. If something should rightly disturb us and trouble our consciences, it is the fact that so many of our brothers and sisters are living without the strength, light and consolation born of friendship with Jesus Christ, without a community of faith to support them, without meaning and a goal in life. More than by fear of going astray, my hope is that we will be moved by the fear of remaining shut up within structures which give us a false sense of security, within rules which make us harsh judges, within habits which make us feel safe, while at our door people are starving and Jesus does not tire of saying to us: 'Give them something to eat' (Mk 6:37).[19]

Among the many privileges of my life as Bishop of Liverpool is the opportunity to meet Christians who are poor, and who from their poverty are sharing extraordinary spiritual riches. This is true for example of our inner urban congregations, and in the same way it is true of Open Table. This group of people has been marginalised and frequently despised, and yet they remain faithful, supporting not only one another but also those in the wider world who suffer the same pains of exclusion and hurt.

The experience of Open Table is not the only experience of LGBTI+ Christians in Liverpool. I have spoken here too with people who feel called in their own lives to observe and to advocate for the traditional teachings of the Church and to conform their own behaviour to these teachings in perpetuity. 'This is a path of great faithfulness, travelled often under the weight of a very heavy cross.'[20] I respect it, as I respect any freely-accepted embracing of celibacy by those, across all the long history of the Church, who have been called to it. But I must also respect the experience of those who feel, after a great deal of prayer and reflection, that their sexuality is a gift from God, to be celebrated as any gift is celebrated. I respect this all the more if it exists in the context of a commitment as Christian disciples to bring the love of Christ to the world and to the broken poor.

How wholeheartedly will we respond to the frequently repeated injunction to listen to the experience of LGBTI people? In my own case, as I listen to that experience across the Diocese, how am I also to listen to the love of God as the Christians of Open Table receive and share it, and as those like them in every diocese and in every city receive and share love? And what then must we do? It is with these questions that I continue to wrestle as a pastor and as a Bishop. It is these questions, heard in the light of the experience of Peter in the Scripture, which God addresses to me. Indeed, it is because of these questions that I have come to believe that we need to change the Church – to make room and to open and extend the table. How we might do so is the matter for our ongoing conversation. But that we should do so is evident to me.

To paraphrase Dr Martin Luther King, 'the arc of Scripture is long, but it bends towards justice'. That was Peter's experience, and as I sit at the open table it is proving to be mine.

Little dogs?

The general point I am wanting to make is that the table of the poor carpenter is an open table where truth comes from the edge. In making it I have spoken at length about the things we may learn from our LGBTI+/Queer friends and companions, partly because I do not often hear that specific point made. The point is not that we should be 'accepting', still less 'tolerant' of these or of any other children of God, but that we should sit and learn more from all on the edge of things, about the One who emptied himself.

In a later sermon at Open Table Liverpool I spoke of the encounter of Jesus with the woman of Syro-Phoenicia, reported to us by St Matthew:

> From there, Jesus went to the regions of Tyre and Sidon. A Canaanite woman from those territories came out and shouted, 'Show me mercy, Son of David. My daughter is suffering terribly from demon possession.' But he didn't respond to her at all.

His disciples came and urged him, 'Send her away; she keeps shouting out after us.'

Jesus replied, 'I've been sent only to the lost sheep, the people of Israel.' But she knelt before him and said, 'Lord, help me. 'He replied, 'It is not good to take the children's bread and toss it to dogs.' She said, 'Yes, Lord. But even the dogs eat the crumbs that fall off their masters' table.' Jesus answered, 'Woman, you have great faith. It will be just as you wish.' And right then her daughter was healed.[21]

In this story Jesus himself in his humanity is challenged and expanded, just as in the story from Acts Peter is challenged and expanded. He visits the borderlands, the region of Tyre. He is met by a woman 'from those boundaries', as Matthew's Greek puts it. On the borders of his experience and of his sympathy, following the vector of the Gospel which is towards openness, he is led now to a radical openness.

He does not answer her perfectly proper request. The disciples urge him to send her away, to remove the disruption, to turn from emptiness and desolation. He speaks of her exclusion, as one from the boundaries, beyond the family of the Jews. He speaks harshly to her. Despite all this she doesn't cease asking him for help, and the self-emptied One is changed by the encounter.

He says 'It is not good to take the children's bread and toss it to dogs' – the Greek is *kunariois*, little dogs, household pets. His first message to her is that she has a place, but it's to be beneath the table, silent, submissive, hungry. Know your place. Or we'll kick you.

But the greatness of the woman's faith overcomes all this rejection. And Jesus recognises it as greatness; 'O woman, great is your faith'. I turn away from the interpretations of this passage that portray Jesus as gently teasing the woman, knowing all along what he would do. For me this story is transformative for the Christian direction of travel, and transformative for Jesus in his humanity. It is transformative for the establishment of the open table, and for the lifting up of those previously seen as little dogs to the place of honour at the table itself.

Christianity as a Way was born and grew in a bustling religious marketplace. The distinctives of the Way arose not from the fact that the Christians had a belief system – everyone had one of those – but from the living of their lives. And the inclusion of this story in the scriptures is one of many signposts to that Way.

As Bishop Peter Price says, 'Christians practised a lifestyle based on shared resources and loving relationships – behaviour quite alien to the people among whom they lived. Their religion understood God as a loving, caring parent; Jesus as beloved son; and themselves as sisters and brothers.'[22] And Roland Walls spoke of building his own community in the way of the self-emptying One 'around silence, solitude, but also an open house with hospitality and a "no label" humanity'.[23]

The application of this passage, and of this chapter as a whole, should not need to be underlined, were it not for the evidence all around us that as Christians we still prefer to travel in another direction. We hear an often-deafening silence in many parts of the church, by no means only in the United States, in the face of growing populist racism and white supremacy. We continue to see an at-best-grudging acceptance in many churches across the world of LGBTI+ people – provided they know their place as little dogs beneath the table, provided that they behave themselves there.

God took the risk

In the face of these things I am nourished by the story of the then Bishop of California (that is of the San Francisco Bay Area) in the 1980s, who was taken to task for supporting those, mostly gay men, who had contracted HIV/AIDS. And when he was told not to be so welcoming of sinners, he is said to have replied: 'God took the risk of becoming a human being; why can't you?'

God took the risk of becoming a human being; and in the story from Matthew we see the incarnate God living that risk, and learning from the poor, from a woman outside the family with a sick child, who endured rejection and who came to be beloved and to see healing in her family. And in the Acts story we see a fisherman following the carpenter who showed him that Way.

And in our own story, is that not to be the journey too? To the open table and from it – from the self-emptying Saviour who made it, to the dignity of those for so long stigmatised as little dogs, emerging from under the table to sit in the honoured seats alongside the poor carpenter who invites them there. Seated in honour beside all who will sit there in honour, an honour none of us deserves, the free gift of eternal grace. Then and for the forever future, and also today. Laughing and rejoicing that justice has finally been brought to victory.

Part III

9. The breakfast table

'You must sit down', says Love, 'and taste my meat': So I did sit and eat.[1]

And then we gathered around that table. And there was more singing and standing, and someone was putting a piece of fresh, crumbly bread in my hands, saying 'the body of Christ', and handing me the goblet of sweet wine, saying 'the blood of Christ', and then something outrageous and terrifying happened. Jesus happened to me.[2]

Jesus said to them, 'Come and have breakfast'.[3]

It's a table for eating

The West London University Chaplaincy, where I worked in the early 1980s, had no church building. We met in halls of residence, in departments, in borrowed vicarages – almost sixty small groups a week, each facilitated by a chaplain or a senior student or a member of staff. Every group met around a table, over a meal. The students took it in turns to bring the food. The tables, we borrowed.

I would carry the practical resources for my groups from place to place in a bulky shoulder-bag. It contained an electric kettle, teabags and coffee, a set of plastic cups, knives (for spreading Marmite or cream cheese or pâté), at least one Bible, a copy of the Alternative Service Book – and a small wooden box containing a small cup and a small plate which my father-in-law, an accomplished silversmith, had made. Everything we needed to resource the church was in that shoulder-bag. But in a real sense, if we had not used the contents of the small wooden box, there would have been nothing worthwhile there.

All the images of the table in this book are resolved in, or imply, or presuppose the Holy Eucharist, the meal that Jesus gave his friends at the table, the meal we have eaten there ever since. And so I want to end my reflections here; at the last supper, at the first breakfast.

Christians connect with God at least as much through their mouths as through their ears. We begin our human life in utter dependence, fed by the pure gift of others; and when we are born again, in utter dependence we are fed again, by the pure gift of grace, at the table of the Lord. In a faith built on the incarnation, it must be so.

I learnt my Eucharistic theology at college. Queen's Birmingham was and is an ecumenical foundation, and in my days there, in the late 1970s, we enjoyed a regular exchange with the local Roman Catholic seminary, Oscott College. The exchange programme was led from Oscott's side by Fr Pat Kelly, an outstanding priest who later became Archbishop of Liverpool. His teaching was rich and helpful, but what I remember most about Fr Pat was his involvement with the local L'Arche community and his enthusiasm for Eucharistic celebrations with people with profound learning disabilities, people for whom conceptual thinking was not an option, people nonetheless who worshipped the Lord their God with all their strength. The seriousness and devotion with which the L'Arche residents received Communion showed me a way. The memory – of devotion richly expressed without concept, of hands held and smiles shared and love extended – remains for me a model of what it can be to be close to the One who said 'I am the Lord your God, who brought you up from Egypt's land. Open your mouth wide—I will fill it up!'[4]

Libraries of books have been written about the Eucharist, about its meanings, its history, the way we should celebrate it today. I do not have the space or the skill to add to them here. But I am glad that I have been given a meal in which to meet God.

A recurrent theme of this book has been that we are not disembodied intellects but people of flesh, and that this is to be celebrated; not simply accepted, and certainly not regretted. Try as we may to be in control of this mysterious concrete world, try as we may to treat God as a brain-puzzle and to solve God with our self-conscious and serious systems, our efforts are doomed to failure. The messiness of the fluid world will defeat us. But this need not depress us or distress us, because we can open our mouths and eat. God is, as God is in Jesus, so there is hope. Jesus will touch and kiss our bloodless lips, too, and make us whole.

Breakfast at the fire

In Virginia Theological Seminary, outside in the garden between the library and the classrooms, is a small bronze sculpture. It portrays the risen Jesus, crouching down at a fire. In his hand he holds a forked stick, and on the end of the stick is a fish. He is cooking the fish at the fire. His face is intent, focused on the task of preparing food for his friends.

The sculpture illustrates the final scene of the Gospel of John, the only one of the four gospels that does not contain the story of the Last Supper:

> Early in the morning, Jesus stood on the shore, but the disciples didn't realize it was Jesus.
>
> Jesus called to them, 'Children, have you caught anything to eat?'
>
> They answered him, 'No.'
>
> He said, 'Cast your net on the right side of the boat and you will find some.' So they did, and there were so many fish that they couldn't haul in the net. Then the disciple whom

Jesus loved said to Peter, 'It's the Lord!' When Simon Peter heard it was the Lord, he wrapped his coat around himself (for he was naked) and jumped into the water. The other disciples followed in the boat, dragging the net full of fish, for they weren't far from shore, only about one hundred yards. When they landed, they saw a fire there, with fish on it, and some bread. Jesus said to them, 'Bring some of the fish that you've just caught.' Simon Peter got up and pulled the net to shore. It was full of large fish, one hundred and fifty-three of them. Yet the net hadn't torn, even with so many fish. Jesus said to them, 'Come and have breakfast.'.[5]

Life is where death was. Fishermen with no fish, followers with no hope. And then daybreak, and abundance, and breakfast. There is no table of wood in this story of bread and fish by the lakeside, but John is writing of the table nonetheless, the table that's for eating, the one I tried to describe in the sermon I preached: *'And if you eat the food served here you will never be hungry again. Because the poor man offers the food at this table. And the poor man will serve you, and the poor man's hands are wounded when he serves you, because the food came at a price, and he paid the price.'*

Jesus, the incarnate Human One, had nowhere to lay his head. He was the guest at so many tables in the days of his life on earth. Now in his risen life he is the host; here at the lakeside, and wherever the food in his memory is served. The command to remember was first given to his friends at a supper. But the meal he always serves today is breakfast, the meal that breaks the fast, that feeds all who are faint with hunger, that releases his friends into a new world of truthfulness and joy.

'When Simon Peter heard it was the Lord, he wrapped his coat around himself (for he was naked) and jumped into the water.' This is a wonderful, comic picture. Commenting on it the great Methodist scholar Kingsley Barrett says drily: 'It is customary, when going for a swim, to take clothes off rather than to put them on.'[6] But in the culture of the time, to greet someone properly you needed to be properly dressed. Peter wanted to do things right – and also to get there fast. He does ridiculous things, to reach his friend quickly and to greet his Lord properly, to sit alongside Jesus again, dripping wet.

This complex motivation – informal honesty in a meal of friends mixed with reverence in the presence of a saving sacrifice – has been the flavour of the Christian Eucharist ever since. Some have tried to eliminate the informality, others the reverence. But the divine breakfast is irreducible. It can neither be reduced to a cultic act, nor to an everyday snack. How could it be, if it speaks of the One who is fully human and fully divine? The comedy of the fully-clothed, soaked disciple catches what it is to be with the God who prepares food for you, and what it is to sit with him and eat.

Yes, most of all it's a table for eating. You can't eat alone at this table. You can't buy a meal at this table. You can't buy a ticket to sit here. Anyone can sit here. It's a table like a table at a wedding. You sit with guests you never knew, and you find out about them, and they become your friends. And the table is spread with a beautiful fair white linen cloth and if you come here, like any pilgrim coming into a new house, they will clothe you in the most beautiful clothes and they will make you welcome.

Meet, drink, watch, stretch

Once again Peter sits alongside the poor carpenter – then at the table, now at the fire. Once again, he is fed by the One who turned and looked at him in his moment of betrayal[7], and who loves him still. In the strength of the food that Jesus gives, Peter is called to face some truths about himself, about the depth of his love, about his future as a disciple, about the way he will glorify God. We are told that the truth hurts him. But it does not disqualify him from ministry. Peter is loved as he is. He is commissioned to feed the hungry with the food that lasts. And then he is told that he will stretch.

> Jesus said to him, 'Feed my sheep. I assure you that when you were younger you tied your own belt and walked around wherever you wanted. When you grow old, you will stretch out your hands and another will tie your belt and lead you where you don't want to go.' He said this to show the kind of death by which Peter would glorify God. After saying this, Jesus said to Peter, 'Follow me.'[8]

The meeting, and drinking, and watching, and stretching of which I have tried to speak are there by the lakeside, just as we too are there. In his ludicrous and glorious humanity, Peter stands for us all; the foolish rock on whom Jesus has built the Church, surrounded by the foolish people whose stony lives add to the cairn of witness to the dancing, living God. At the table where Peter sat, we sit. At the fire where Peter ate, we eat. After saying this, Jesus said to Peter, 'Follow me'. After saying this, Jesus says to me, 'Follow me'. After saying this, Jesus says to you, 'Follow me'.

Appendix

The undefended table: a provocation

Taste and see...[1]

Perhaps people's opinions settle so strongly on the altar because they believe it is the only meeting point between human and divine desire. But it's also the place from which the meal at the center of the Eucharist is served. In other words, it's a table.[2]

Just after I preached the sermon which stands at the beginning of this book, the parish of Holy Trinity Formby, in the Diocese of Liverpool, commissioned a new altar. It is composed of four smaller tables, which when brought together form a single large table around the edge of which these words are written: 'The table of the poor man; the table of the King'. When the tables are separated, each one of the smaller tables is found to have these same words written around it: The table | of the poor man | The table | of the King. The idea is that the same table that focused the community of Christ in worship at the Eucharist will then be dispersed to serve the wider community, perhaps as tables at a street party, or tables covered with essential provisions for dispersal from the food bank. After some interesting negotiation with the Diocesan Advisory Committee who are responsible for approving innovations like this, I am delighted that Formby's approach has prevailed and the altar is good to go.

Halfway around the world from Formby, in Potrero Hill, San Francisco, the same impulse is at work. Paul Fromberg writes:

> The altar at the center of St Gregory's worship is a semi-round, wooden table. It is regularly used for blessing bread and wine, but it is also used for other things. I use it as a work table sometimes. Other times we use it as the centrepiece for our weekly food pantry. After the service on Sundays, we serve our refreshments on it and keep the Eucharistic celebration going with coffee and tea. We can use the table this way because we

are clear about what it is: when we vest it, covering it with a colourful cloth, it is the mystical eating-point between God and us. When we uncover it, it's the place where we swap stories or organise the choir folders. It's a functional table, on the same level as the people, not lifted up on a platform behind an altar rail. It is a place that is designed to include everyone.

And he goes on:

The table of the Eucharistic meal has to be one to which everyone is welcome, not just because we want to be inclusive but because we want to be made real.[3]

I'm writing this in an Anglican monastery in New York State, on the day that the Episcopal Church remembers John and Charles Wesley. The departure of the Methodist people from the Church of England, the failure of the Anglican leadership of the time to make and keep room for them, remains a wasteful wound in the body of Christ. The Wesleys drank deeply from the fountain of scripture, creeds and early church writers, as their own writings and hymns make evident.

The monastery in which I write this, which is remembering the Wesleys today, has a simple, calm style of Anglican catholic worship, evident especially in its celebration of the Eucharist. At the moment of receiving communion the rubric of their liturgy says, 'all are welcome to receive'. In a Cathedral in another part of the USA the message is: 'Everyone, without exception, is invited to receive Communion.'

The following liturgical invitation, from San Diego, goes into a little more detail:

All who seek God are welcome to the Lord's Table to receive the Bread and Wine. Even if you do not seek God, God seeks you. Come and hold in your hand and taste on your lips the love which we cannot comprehend.[4]

As does this from San Francisco:

Jesus welcomes everyone to his Table, so we offer Communion, Christ's Body and Blood, to everyone and to everyone by name.[5]

Forms of words similar to those above, with a similar approach to the table of Christ, are to be found in Church of England churches too. Others use words of invitation along these lines without actively intending to extend Eucharistic hospitality beyond the community of the baptised. I know of no Anglican church that conducts weekly a sustained examination of those offering themselves at the table before sharing the bread and wine with them.

Meanwhile the law of the Church speaks with a different tone. In the USA the canons of the Episcopal Church are clear enough:

No unbaptized person shall be eligible to receive Holy Communion in this Church.[6]

The Church of England has a more complex approach which more or less says the same thing, so long as it is understood that 'membership of the Church of England' is an agreed category which presupposes baptism[7]:

1. There shall be admitted to the Holy Communion:
(a) members of the Church of England who have been confirmed in accordance with the rites of that Church or are ready and desirous to be so confirmed or who have been otherwise episcopally confirmed with unction or with the laying on of hands except as provided by the next following Canon;
(b) baptized persons who are communicant members of other Churches which subscribe to the doctrine of the Holy Trinity, and who are in good standing in their own Church;
(c) any other baptized persons authorized to be admitted under regulations of the General Synod; and
(d) any baptized person in immediate danger of death.[8]

Neither of these canons is designed to be a liturgical invitation, and indeed they would make poor ones, though it is hard to see how the C of E one can be easily abridged, if you should want to communicate its meaning within a service of worship.

You can, however, spin the meaning of these canons so that they communicate warmth, In my own days as a parish priest, now fifteen years ago, I would use some such form as 'We welcome to receive Communion those who are full members of any church'. I have heard others say something like: 'We welcome all baptised Christians to the Lord's table this morning'. Though invitations like these do not cover all the bases laid out in Canon B15A, they make a point that not everyone is to be admitted. I went on, as many do, to explain that all who wished were warmly welcome to come to the altar for a blessing, and gave some stage directions for the benefit of the distributors of the elements, for example inviting people to cross their arms in front of them, or to carry a booklet in their hands, or something of the kind.

I have heard other and shorter invitations which focus on a different criterion, namely the internal state of the recipient, so something like: 'We welcome to receive Communion all who love the Lord Jesus', or '...all who wish to draw close to Jesus'. This is uncanonical, like just about every other invitation I have ever heard. But it is certainly warmer than the Canon itself.

Back to John Wesley. Speaking of course into a culture where almost everyone was baptised as a matter of course, he took a more evangelistic view of the Sacrament. A report presented to the British Methodist Conference in 2003 says this:

> On the grounds of experience Wesley declared that there were those who owed the very beginning of their conversion to God to what God had worked in them at the Lord's Supper: it was a 'converting ordinance'. The teaching of the Wesleys was that Communion could lead a genuine seeker first to find Christ, then to be justified by believing faith and finally through constant attendance at the Lord's Supper and the other means of grace to reach a state of scriptural holiness and entire sanctification in heart and life, having been made perfect in love.

I assume Wesley was saying that participation in the Eucharist can convert nominal faith, the background radiation of Christendom, into real faith. How can we in our generation make sense of his perception? Our context today is very different from his. In these days by no means everyone has been baptised. Moreover today in many churches the Eucharist is the normal, often the only, service of worship on offer. The missional context has changed beyond recognition, and I wonder whether this has caught the churches of the postmodern West napping.

At any rate the provocation is this: if we believe that the poor carpenter welcomes all to sit and eat, why may we not extend that invitation, and extend a serving of the meal at his table, to the unbaptised? If this table holds the meal of freely given grace, the meal that both reminds and enacts our communion with Christ, then why is it only available to those who already know him; to baptised Christians? Why must this table, of all tables, be defended?

I describe this appendix as a provocation, because I myself have been provoked by the implications for our worship and life of an undefended table. It seems to me that the matter should be shared and aired.

The underground stream of the church, as I have indicated a number of times in this book, comes through the witness of those on the edge of things. I also note that it has very often come through the witness of women, whose credibility and legitimacy in the church has often been questioned, and is frequently questioned still. A living example of this is the witness of Sara Miles, who until recently worked at St Gregory's church in San Francisco and whose books *Take This Bread* and *Jesus Freak* have brought the Gospel of grace to tens of thousands of people in our generation.

Take This Bread contains her testimony, the testimony of one who knew little to nothing of the habits of worship of the church. I have quoted her words at the beginning of the last chapter; an unbaptised seeker in an unfamiliar place – '*...and someone was putting a piece of fresh, crumbly bread in my hands, saying "the body of Christ", and handing me the goblet of sweet wine, saying "the blood of Christ", and then something outrageous and terrifying happened. Jesus happened to me*'. She goes on to describe her shock as she realised that '*God, named "Christ" or "Jesus", was real and in my mouth – [it] utterly short-circuited my ability to do anything but cry*'.[9]

There are many testimonies to the transforming power of worship. I myself have one, and I told it earlier – the compelling impact of a dancer's devotion on a lost and hungry visitor. But Sara

Miles' testimony provokes me further, because if she had visited my church in England, and if I had known her background beforehand, then I would not have offered her bread and wine, but I would have invited her 'to receive a blessing'. She would have received a touch and heard good words, but nothing would have been real and in her mouth.

It is, to put it mildly, theologically contentious to ask whether centuries of Christian liturgical tradition should be overturned by giving Communion to the unbaptised.[10] For many, an undefended table would constitute one more step in the direction of a theologically vacuous religion, uncaring of the need for repentance and conversion of life. And I strongly agree that, like anything we do in the Church, we should establish good reasons for the way we invite people to share the body and blood of the Lord; that is for the way we exercise what Philip Turner calls our 'working theology' in this area of our life.

In the United States the Episcopal Church has been formally addressing this matter since 2006. In the UK the matter has never come to the conscious public attention of the House of Bishops or the General Synod as far as I know.

But in a post-Christendom Europe, where the language of the faith is increasingly absent from the common cultural store, where becoming a Christian is commonly misunderstood by people as a process of intellectual and philosophical assent and nothing more, I remain provoked by the example of the undefended table. I am not so far provoked that I have an answer to the questions raised by this practice, and I am not so far provoked as to want to embrace it unilaterally. But it seems to me time that this question should be addressed in England. To do so we will need of course to refer to liturgical history and to explore what our sacramental practice says about our theology of salvation, and about the relation of the sacrament of holy baptism to the sacrament of the holy Eucharist. But if we truly are a missional people we will need to be open to other questions too. For example 'What might God be calling us to do now, in this cultural context, to feed those who are hungry for his life?' And, 'How may we live at peace with the invitations we so easily make, week by week, to people to come and share in the life of God at the table of the poor carpenter?'

Salvation is offered to the broken. 'For while we were still weak', says St Paul, 'at the right time Christ died for the ungodly. Indeed, rarely will anyone die for a righteous person—though perhaps for a good person someone might actually dare to die. But God proves his love for us in that while we still were sinners Christ died for us.'[11]

Fundamentally and finally I am provoked by this: Jesus wants all the world to receive his love and his salvation. The Bible tells us that he emptied himself, and was therefore exalted. But it does not seem to me that in his exaltation, he has filled himself again. There is a poor man in heaven, whose glorious body bears forever the marks of One who became sin for me. And I do not believe that our Lord is defensive of his dignity, he who was crucified outside the walls and who identified himself with Isaiah's servant, giving up his face to shame and spitting. If this is the God I worship, should I not treat the gifts he has entrusted to me in the same spirit that he himself treated them, and give them away freely to any and all who ask? I'm a follower of Jesus; poor and broken, he's my king. And as the saying goes: 'You mustn't be more of a royalist than the king.'[12]

I'll end this appendix, and this book, with a word-picture. It speaks of a service of worship in a field. It speaks of God's love, to me.

> I chanted the Eucharistic prayer, and people took the bread and wine and shared them freely with the neo-hippie carnival performers and the black grandmothers, the post-evangelicals and the southern Evangelicals, the queers and the frat boys, the babies and the elders. You know—it was like church.[13]

Notes

Acknowledgements

[1] In the Calendar of the Episcopal Church.

1. So there's this table

[1] In the inauguration service the new bishop is given a cope and mitre, and preaches wearing these.

[2] Tracey Emin is a contemporary British artist whose neon installation, 'I felt you and I knew you loved me', is fixed over the west doors of Liverpool Cathedral.

[3] The Most Revd Malcolm McMahon, Roman Catholic Archbishop of Liverpool.

[4] The Revd Phil Jump, Baptist Regional Minister for the North-West.

[5] In 1989, ninety-six football fans were killed at Hillsborough, Sheffield, England. The fans were widely blamed for their own deaths. Their families have struggled for nearly thirty years to clear their names, and a recent inquest has indeed cleared them. My predecessor as Bishop of Liverpool, James Jones, chaired an investigatory panel which made an enormous contribution to this result.

[6] David Sheppard was an inspirational Bishop of Liverpool and a key influence on the commitment of the Church of England to the urban life of the nation and to those on the edge of things. See his book *Bias to the Poor* (1983) and the C of E report *Faith in the City* (1985).

2. The banqueting table

[1] Song of Songs 2:4; lyric translation by Kevin Prosch, 'His banner over me'.

[2] Richard Fabian, *Founding Principles of St Gregory of Nyssa*, 1978.

[3] Julian of Norwich, *Revelations of Divine Love*, chapter 86.

[4] In *Orthodox Perspectives on Mission*

[5] 1 Corinthians 8:2, 3. The Bible version used in this book is the Common English Bible unless otherwise stated.

[6] The words of a young Confirmation candidate in Warrington, who was asked to describe her faith.

[7] Luke 19:1-10.

[8] Luke 7:36-50.

[9] Luke 11:37ff.

[10] John Dominic Crossan, *Jesus: A Revolutionary Biography*, pp. 74, 77.

[11] Luke 15:2. Fabian comments, 'The Greek οὗτος ["this one"] is pejorative and dismissive. Hence, "this guy".'

[12] St Isaac of Nineveh, *Spiritual Homilies*.

[13] In John 10:11, Jesus says, 'I am the shepherd the "kalos".' The Greek word *kalos* can mean 'good' and it can also mean 'beautiful'. This idea comes from William Temple, *Reflections on St John's Gospel*.

[14] This prayer is used at the beginning of each service in that church.

3. The Lord's table

[1] Evelyn Underhill, in a letter to the Archbishop of Canterbury, 1930.

[2] Acts 17:24-28.

[3] Matthew 28:20.

[4] John 1:18.

[5] 1 Kings 19.

6   Aelred Squire, *Asking the Fathers*, p.147.
7   Ezekiel 47:9.
8   Julian of Norwich, *Revelations of Divine Love*, ch. 133.
9   Julian of Norwich, *Revelations of Divine Love*, ch. 64.
10 Matthew 7:13.
11 'Fundamentalism and Wonder' [https://www.theamericanconservative.com/dreher/fundamentalism-wonder-awe/comment-page-2/]
12 Edwin Muir, 'The Incarnate One'.
13 Isaiah 45:15.
14 1 Timothy 3:16.
15 John 1:26.
16 Gregory of Nyssa, *The Life of Moses*.
17 *Cloud of Unknowing*, chapter 6.
18 Aelred Squire, *Asking the Fathers*, p.xx.
19 *On Prayer*, 60 (P. G. 79, 1180B).

4. The daily table

1   John 7:17.
2   Ursula K. Le Guin, *The Lathe of Heaven*.
3   Ezekiel 47:1–6a.
4   See e.g. Acts 18:25, 24:14, 24:22
5   In William Sewell, *The History of the Rise, Increase and Progress of the Christian People Called Quakers* (New York, 1844), pp. 202, 203.
6   Tracey Emin in Liverpool Cathedral; see the chapter 'So there's this table' above.
7   Alan Jones, *Reimagining Christianity*, p.72.
8   Martyn Percy, *Anglicanism: Confidence, Commitment and Communion*, Ashgate 2013, p. 7. Percy is drawing on the thinking of Etienne Wenger.
9   James 1:27.
10 Samuel Beckett, 'Worstward Ho'.
11 Colossians 1:28.
12 1 Corinthians 9:24.
13 Hebrews 1:8, 9.
14 Matthew 11:30.

5. Meeting at the table

Friends of God

1   John 15:12–17.
2   St Gregory Nazianzen, *The Song of His Life*, p. 324
3   1 John 3:14.
4   C. S. Lewis, *The Four Loves*, p.73.
5   In Humphrey Carpenter, *The Inklings*.
6   Sallie McFague, quoted in Elisabeth Moltmann-Wendel, *Rediscovering Friendship*, p. 9.
7   Proverbs 27:6 (King James Version).
8   Martin Buber, in *I and Thou* (Ronald Gregor Smith's translation).
9   Aelred of Rievaulx, *Christian Friendship*, p.75.
10 He is quoting Cicero, *Christian Friendship*, p.36.
11 C. S. Lewis, *The Four Loves*, p. 69.
12 Kenneth Child, *In His Own Parish*, p.15.
13 Alan Bennett, 'Take a Pew', from *Beyond the Fringe*, 1961.
14 Monica Furlong, *C of E: The state it's in*, p.252.
15 People who have grown accustomed to hearing Jesus refer to himself in the Gospels as 'the Son of Man' may find this jarring. Why 'Human One'? Jesus' primary language would have been Aramaic, so he would have used the Aramaic phrase *bar enosha*. This phrase has the sense of 'a human' or 'a human such as I...' The value of this translation

is further debated here: https://www.biblegateway.com/blog/2011/08/son-of-man-or-human-one-tough-translation-questions-raised-by-the-common-english-bible/

16   Luke 7:33-35.
17   Jürgen Moltmann, *The Open Church*, p.51.
18   *The Open Church*, p.61.
19   *The Open Church*, p.51.
20   *The Open Church*, p.51.
21   *The Open Church*, p.51.
22   *The Open Church*, p.52.
23   Galatians 3:28.
24   *The Open Church*, p.53.
25   The Open Church, p.62.
26   Jerry Ryan, *National Catholic Reporter*, November 2008.
27   Carlo Carretto, *I Sought and I Found*, p.37.
28   Carlo Carretto, *I Sought and I Found*, p.34.

Jesus' group in Jesus' time

1   John 10:14. My own translation.
2   John 1:14.
3   John 3:11.
4   In fact 49 per cent. Assessed by Jim Egli, and quoted by Bill Beckham in *The Second Reformation*, p.181.
5   Mark 3:13-15.
6   Acts 1:15-16, 21-23.
7   John 3:11.
8   Luke 18:22-23.
9   Lesslie Newbigin, *The Gospel in a Plural Society*, p.227.
10   Adolf Harnack, *The Mission and Expansion of Christianity*, 1906.
11   1 John 1:1-3.
12   You may believe, as some do, that 1 John was not written by that John. This would make my point even more clearly; the writer is able to identify completely with Jesus' group, which has already extended to include him/her.
13   John 17:20-23.
14   Luke 4:38.
15   2 Corinthians 12:2-4.
16   Galatians 1:15-17.
17   Acts 15:36-40.
18   2 Peter 3:15-17.
19   Acts 9:17-19, 26.
20   1 Corinthians 2:12-13. Many thanks to Dr Paula Gooder for this reference.
21   Acts 17:14,15.
22   Acts 17:34.
23   Acts 20:36-38.
24   Acts 28:30, 31.

Jesus' group today

1   Romans 1:1,7; 15:24
2   Roman Catholic Archdiocese of Vitoria, Brazil: 'The Church the People Want'. Included in David Prior, *The Church in the Home*.
3   John 20:26-31.
4   Graham Pulkingham, *To Know and Be Known*.
5   David Ford, *Self and Salvation*, p. 159.
6   Matthew 18:19-22.

7   A besetting sin of small-group life in church is to describe the multiplying of a group as 'splitting'. A group splitting sounds like a disaster. A group multiplying is the opposite of disaster; it is the very fulfilment of the purpose of the group.

8   Martin Buber, *I and Thou*, trans. Walter Kaufmann, T & T Clark, 1970.

9   *I and Thou*, p. 85.

10 *I and Thou*, p. 62. (The phrase 'All real living is meeting' is from Ronald Gregor Smith's older translation.)

11 See the church website at http://houseforall.org. I shall say more about the phrase 'queer-inclusive' later.

12 1 Corinthians 14:40 (King James Version).

13 This is my own translation. See *I and Thou*, p. 69.

14 Robert D. Putnam, *Bowling Alone: The Collapse and Revival of American Community*, 2000.

15 The story is told in Michael Harper, *A New Way of Living*, out of print now but available via http://www.communityofcelebration.com/Books/anwol.pdf

16 David Watson, *You Are my God*.

17 Michael Hollings, *Living Priesthood*.

18 See Michael Ramsey, *The Christian Priest Today*, p. 50.

19 Isaiah 25:8, Revelation 7:17, 21:4.

20 Luke 5:3-10.

21 John 4:6-9, 19, 28-30.

22 Luke 19:5, 6, 8.

23 Genesis 3:10.

24 Graham Pulkingham, *To Know and be Known*, p.161.

25 Matthew 26:49, 50.

26 Matthew 6:2, 5, 17.

27 Hebrews 10:24, 25.

28 2 Corinthians 12:9.

29 2 Timothy 2:24 (Authorised Version).

30 John 15:16.

31 Thomas Merton, *Day of a Stranger*.

32 See Gresford Chitemo, 'The East African Revival', appendix to D. F. Wells, *God the Evangelist*.

33 In interview, Kingdom Power Trust video, *Healing Prayer*.

34 Martin Buber, 'Dialogue', in *Between Man and Man*, p.33.

35 Romans 4:17.

36 From Geoffrey Hill, 'Three Mystical Songs' (The Pentecost Castle), in *Agenda* magazine, 1974.

37 Ruth Burrows, *Guidelines for Mystical Prayer*, p.88.

38 Rowan Williams, *The Wound of Knowledge*, p.175.

39 Luke 14:28-30.

40 The full text is in the *Methodist Covenant Service*.

41 A version given to me by John Halsey of the Community of the Transfiguration, Roslin, Midlothian.

42 Graham Pulkingham, *They Left Their Nets*, pp. 29-30.

6. Drinking from the fountain

1   John 4:13, 14.

2   John 7:37-39.

3   Lao Tzu, Tao Te Ching, 8:1, Translated by James Legge.

4   Matthew 18:1-5.

5   Michael Ramsey, *The Gospel and the Catholic Church,* Kindle loc. 1944-1948.

6   George Lindbeck, *The Nature of Doctrine*, p. 132.

7   Leander Keck, summarising his research article 'The premodern Bible in the postmodern world'.

8   2 Timothy 3:16.

⁹   See http://archive.churchsociety.org/crossway/documents/Cway_081_Allister12.pdf

¹⁰   Frances Young, *Virtuoso Theology*, p.159.

¹¹   Doctrine Commission of the Church of England, *Christian Believing*, 1976, p. 3.

¹²   p. 19.

¹³   Doctrine Commission of the Church of England, *Believing in the Church*, 1981.

¹⁴   Dorothy L. Sayers, *The Just Vengeance* – the Lichfield Morality Play for 1946.

¹⁵   Stuart Townend and Keith Getty, © 2001 Thankyou Music.

¹⁶   https://www.psephizo.com/biblical-studies/did-jesus-die-to-satisfy-gods-wrath/

7. Watching in the moment

¹   Thomas Merton, *Conjectures of a Guilty Bystander*, p. xx.

²   These ideas build on those in the fine book by Aelred Squire, *Asking the Fathers*, SPCK

³   https://christdesert.org/prayer/rule-of-st-benedict/chapter-20-reverence-in-prayer/

⁴   Teresa of Avila, Way of Perfection, chapter 22.

⁵   Ralph Martin, *The Fulfilment of All Desire*, p. 121.

⁶   1 Corinthians 16:22; Revelation 22:20. For more on this see Thomas Keating, *Open Mind, Open Heart*, or John Main, *Word into Silence*.

⁷   For more on this see Kallistos Ware, *The Orthodox Way*, or John Wimber's, *Power Healing*, or Simon Tugwell's *Did you Receive the Spirit?*, or David Pytches', *Come Holy Spirit*.

8. Stretching for the Kingdom

More people knowing Jesus

¹   John 20:28.

²   The Archbishops of Canterbury and York, in the preface to the report of the Evangelism Task Group to the General Synod of the Church of England, February 2016.

³   2 Corinthians 5:14, 15.

⁴   1 Peter 3:14–16.

⁵   SCM Press, 1981.

⁶   The translation is Bishop David Jenkins'. See *The Contradiction of Christianity* (1985).

⁷   Danny Daniels, *Power Evangelism* conference, Edinburgh 1988.

⁸   T. S. Eliot, *Sweeney Agonistes*.

⁹   https://www.theguardian.com/world/2006/may/05/religion.uk

¹⁰   *Metro*, 2 October 2017, http://metro.co.uk/2017/10/02/panic-on-london-train-after-man-reads-passages-from-the-bible-6971519/

¹¹   From Samuel M. Janney, *The Life of William Penn: With Selections from His Correspondence and Auto-Biography*. Philadelphia: Hogan, Perkins, and Co., 1852.

¹²   http://www.anabaptistwitness.org/journal_entry/belong-believe-behave-reflections-on-church-planting-in-germany/

More justice in the world

¹   Isaiah 42:3, quoted in Matthew 12:20 (NRSV).

²   Gordon W. Lathrop, *Holy Ground: A Liturgical Cosmology*, pp. 64–5. I am grateful to Rick Fabian for this reference.

³   *Faith in the City*, 3.29.

⁴   *Faith in the City*, 3.31.

⁵   Charles Péguy, quoted by Dorothy Day in *Aims and Purposes of the Catholic Worker Movement*, 1940.

⁶   Philippians 2:5–11.

⁷   *Theological Dictionary of the New Testament*, ed. Gerhard Kittel.

⁸   Philippians 2:7,8, in David Bentley Hart, *The New Testament*, p. 392.

⁹   Roland Walls and Ron Ferguson, *Mole under the Fence*, p. 6.

¹⁰   Luther, *Complete Sermons*, Vol. 5, p. 473.

¹¹   Isaiah 53:2–6.

12 I owe the title of this section, and many of the ideas in it, to the Revd Liz Edman of New York. See her excellent book *Queer Virtue*, Beacon Press, 2016.

13 Martin Buber, *Tales of the Hasidim*, Vol. 2.

14 Elizabeth M. Edman, *Queer Virtue*, p. 119.

15 *Queer Virtue*, p. 127.

16 Acts 11:5–9.

17 Walter Hollenweger, *Evangelism Today: Good News or Bone of Contention?* (Christian Journals Ltd, Belfast, 1976) p.15.

18 *Evangelism Today*, pp. 16–17.

19 Pope Francis, *Evangelii Gaudium*, para 49.

20 *Issues in Human Sexuality*, 5.5.

21 Matthew 15:21–28. Cf. Mark 7:24–30.

22 Peter Price, *The Kingdom is the Church*.

23 Quoted in John Mantle, *The First Worker-Priests*.

9. The breakfast table

1 George Herbert, 'Love III'.

2 Sara Miles, *Take This Bread*, p.58.

3 John 21:12.

4 Psalm 81:10.

5 John 21:4–12.

6 C. K. Barrett, *The Gospel According to St John: A Commentary on the Greek Text*, p. 580.

7 Luke 22:61.

8 John 21:15–19.

Appendix

The undefended table: a provocation

1 Psalm 34:8.

2 Paul Fromberg, *The Way of Transformation*, p.104.

3 Paul Fromberg, *The Way of Transformation*, pp. 85–6.

4 Quoted by Stephen Edmondson in *Staying One, Remaining Open*, Richard J. Jones and J. Barney Hawkins IV, eds. p. 70.

5 Donald Schell, 'Open Table in Community and Mission', *Anglican Theological Review*, vol. 94, p. 247.

6 Title 1, Canon 17, Section 7.

7 Which is at least debatable. See for example Harriet Harris in the Faith and Order Commission report *The Journey of Christian Initiation* (2011), pp. 54–5: 'The link between baptism and committed membership has weakened in most churches … it is a pastoral concern whether unbaptised sympathisers can and should be treated as members of the church … In short, the notion of membership is vague, as is the status of those who seem neither to be simply within or without the Church.' See also Paul Avis, *The Anglican Understanding of the Church*, pp.15ff.

8 Canon B15A.

9 Sara Miles, *Take This Bread*, pp.58, 59.

10 Many see the question as foolish and dangerous. See for example *An Unworkable Theology* – a brief but powerfully-argued piece by Philip Turner, focusing a distinction between 'those who hold a theology of divine *acceptance* from those who hold a theology of divine *redemption*'. *First Things* magazine, June 2005, pp. 10–12. See also a cautiously negative assessment by Bishop Thomas Breidenthal, 'Following Jesus Outside' in *Anglican Theological Review*, Spring 2012, p. 257, and a more neutral overview in the same volume by Ruth A. Meyers, 'Who may be invited to the table?', p. 233.

11 Romans 5:6–8.

12 Vicomte de Chateaubriand: '*Il ne faut pas être plus royaliste que le Roi.*' In *De la Monarchie selon la Charte* (Paris 1816) LXXXI.

13 Paul Fromberg, *The Art of Transformation*, p. 53.